Stop and Frisk

Every law enforcement patrol officer and investigator needs to understand both the tactical considerations of stopping and frisking a suspect and the legal constraints that should govern that power. Recent years have shown clearly the damage that can be done when police lack an adequate understanding of the legal foundation for their activities. In this new edition of *Stop and Frisk*, Mitchell and Connor team up to provide active or aspiring police officers with the knowledge of applicable law as well as practical techniques they need to safely and legally carry out their crime-suppression and investigative duties. This updated edition includes clear summaries of the major cases of the last decade and the lessons learned when police and communities lacked adequate understanding of the legal foundation of law enforcement activity.

Ideal for in-service training at the post-academy level, this book also gives time-tested tools to police officers, supervisors, and legal advisors. *Stop and Frisk* can be used to teach undergraduate Criminal Justice majors as well as concerned citizens to prevent crime in their communities.

Douglas R. Mitchell, J.D., M.P.A., has been an attorney for 30 years. He is a deputy prosecutor in Washington State, assigned to the Civil Division of his office. His duties include advising several clients in different parts of the Criminal Justice system, and serving as public records officer for the office. He has broad experience in both civil and criminal duties, including the prosecution of violent felons.

He is a graduate of the University of Illinois College of Law and Police Training Institute, and he has been a prosecutor and part-time officer in Illinois and Washington. His primary interest is in the legal foundations of law enforcement operations, and he has authored and co-authored several books and articles on related topics.

Gregory J. Connor, M.S., is Professor Emeritus at the University of Illinois Police Training Institute. For more than four decades he provided both practical and tactical education and training to police officers and corrections personnel.

Professor Connor has published numerous texts and articles on associated topics in the criminal justice field and is a recognized expert on such topics as use of force, contact controls, police pursuits, jail and police procedures and policies, etc.

He is the originator of the Use of Force Model and the recent Police and Jail Control Models designed and developed for peace officers throughout the country and additional graphic illustrations to enhance the training effort in areas including use of force issues, stop and frisk dynamics, vehicle stops, and contemporary operations in both police agencies and jails.

"While the phrase 'every police professional should have this text in their library' is often overused, I have to attach that mindset to this new manual. Right from the opening pages, this 140-page reference book is loaded with relevant material every police trainer, first- or second-line supervisor, and/or academy instructor needs to know."

—David Grossi, Grossi Consulting, Bonita Springs, FL; Irondequoit (NY) Police Department (Lieutenant, retired)

"My experience is that officers who don't understand the concept of investigative detention will do one of two things when confronted by person(s) who are behaving suspiciously: either they will fail to act, diminishing their ability to prevent crime, or act without the proper legal authority, which causes the criminal prosecutor many problems later. Not to mention, we as peace officers have a duty to protect the Constitutional rights of all citizens or inhabitants of every jurisdiction. I would recommend that veteran officers need this text even more than academy cadets. The authors' experience makes this a real world text that will be invaluable to successfully performing a very difficult job."

—Dale Mann, Georgia Command College; retired director, Georgia Peace Officers Standards and Training Council

"Mitchell and Connor have done law enforcement, the legal profession, and—importantly—interested members of the public a tremendous service. In easy-to-understand language, they have explained what types of encounters the public and police can have, the legal standards for them, and best practices for them."

—Sergeant Erick Gelhaus, Sonoma County, CA, Sheriff's Office

"This should be mandatory reading for anyone teaching *Terry* stops to all peace officers, jurists, or prosecutors looking to stay current on this important area of law. It nicely blends the arcane world of legal matters with the gritty humor and wisdom of the street cop."

—Lieutenant Colonel David G. Bolgiano, USAF (retired), author of *Virtuous Policing*

Stop and Frisk

Legal Perspectives, Strategic Thinking, and Tactical Procedures

Third Edition

**Douglas R. Mitchell and
Gregory J. Connor**

NEW YORK AND LONDON

Third edition published 2018
by Routledge
711 Third Avenue, New York, NY 10017

and by Routledge
2 Park Square, Milton Park, Abingdon, Oxon, OX14 4RN

Routledge is an imprint of the Taylor & Francis Group, an informa business

© 2018 Taylor & Francis

The right of Douglas R. Mitchell and Gregory J. Connor to be
identified as authors of this work has been asserted by them in
accordance with sections 77 and 78 of the Copyright, Designs and
Patents Act 1988.

First edition published by Stipes Publishing L.L.C. 2000
Second edition published by Stipes Publishing L.L.C. 2007

Library of Congress Cataloging-in-Publication Data
Names: Mitchell, Douglas R. (Lawyer), author. | Connor,
    Gregory J., author.
Title: Stop and frisk : legal perspectives, strategic thinking, and
    tactical procedures / Douglas R. Mitchell and Gregory J. Connor.
Description: Third edition. | New York, NY : Routledge, 2017. |
    Includes index.
Identifiers: LCCN 2017021206 | ISBN 9781138302945 (hardback) |
    ISBN 9781138302969 (pbk.)
Subjects: LCSH: Stop and frisk (Law enforcement)—Law and
    legislation—United States. | Stop and frisk (Law enforcement)—
    United States.
Classification: LCC KF9630 .M58 2017 | DDC 345.73/052—dc23
LC record available at https://lccn.loc.gov/2017021206

ISBN: 978-1-138-30294-5 (hbk)
ISBN: 978-1-138-30296-9 (pbk)
ISBN: 978-0-203-73158-1 (ebk)

Typeset in Goudy
by Apex CoVantage, LLC

The authors would like to dedicate this text to:

Detective Martin McFadden, Cleveland (OH) Police Department. Without his excellent performance in the initial phases of what would become *Terry v. Ohio*, American law enforcement probably would not have the resulting tool to use to interdict crime and protect the community.

Patrick A. Rogers, Sergeant, NYPD (ret.); CWO2, USMCR (ret.); and so much more: friend, mentor, historian, and teacher. As he said, "Bad guys are bad guys, no matter their plumbing, their accent or how they came out of the paint shop."—(11/18/2013)
RIP, Pat. We are diminished.

Contents

Foreword

On June 19, 1961, the Supreme Court in *Mapp v. Ohio* held that the Fourth Amendment's guarantee—that the "right of the people . . . against unreasonable searches and seizures, shall not be violated"—would henceforth be protected by an exclusionary rule applicable to the conduct of state and local police, just as had theretofore been the case as to federal officials, for otherwise that Amendment would be "reduced to 'a form of words.'" Less than three months later, I began my academic life at the University of Illinois (where I am still ensconced). This coincidence may account for the fact that during the intervening years the main focus of my attention has been the Fourth Amendment, and especially its treatment by the Supreme Court and lower courts, culminating in a treatise now in a six-volume fifth edition. (I have yet to exhaust the subject, but am close to being exhausted *by* the subject!)

I report this only to explain how it is that I have been asked time and again over the years to name the most important post-*Mapp* Fourth Amendment decision of the Supreme Court. Often I have declined to answer, for there are many deserving candidates, and to select one would make it appear that I had overlooked some landmark ruling by the Court. But if I *had* to make a choice, it would doubtless be the Court's 1968 decision in *Terry v. Ohio*, the Court's initial foray into that bedeviling subject today known by the sobriquet "stop and frisk." Before *Terry*, the lower-court decisions on the subject were in disarray: some, for example, viewed the Fourth Amendment's "seizure" characterization as applicable only to a full-fledged to-the-station arrest, thus leaving any lesser intrusion totally ungoverned by the Fourth Amendment, while some others thought that "seizure" encompassed any nonconsensual encounter of a citizen with a police officer *and* that all such seizures were subject to the very same requirement of full "probable cause." In *Terry*, the Court went no further than it had to in order to resolve the case at hand, but in the process developed a sound structure upon which it and lesser courts were able to elaborate on future occasions: between a truly consensual encounter and a full-fledged arrest, the Court recognized an intermediate category of police "seizure" activity permissible upon reasonable suspicion "that criminal activity may be afoot," and incident to such a seizure a "limited search" is justified upon reasonable suspicion that the person "may be armed and dangerous."

From what is now nearly a half century of experience under *Terry*, I believe three conclusions are in order regarding "stop and frisk":

Quite clearly, the authority expressly recognized in Terry and elaborated by the courts during this interval has proven to be a highly valuable law enforcement tool. Were the police, on the other hand, limited to forcible intervention only in those instances when there was already sufficient evidence to justify an arrest and charge, the public interest would be badly served.

Just as clearly, as anyone who reads the daily newspaper has learned, some police (and, indeed, some police departments) have seriously failed to abide by the limits of *Terry* and its progeny. These failures have had grave repercussions and are justifiably a matter of great concern.

Even after all these years, it can sometimes be extremely difficult to determine exactly what the limits of the Terry authority are, as illustrated by a federal appellate court decision just weeks ago on the question of whether the frisk authority is now more limited in light of the Supreme Court's Second Amendment precedents recognizing a right to carry a loaded gun outside of the home. The majority's conclusion (no), because it is illogical to contend that "when a person forcefully stopped may be legally permitted to possess a firearm, any risk of danger to police officers posed by the firearm is eliminated," seem eminently sensible, but then so does the dissenters' objection that the majority's position, taken together with the Supreme Court's longstanding approval of pre-textual traffic stops, creates a great potential for mischief.

Given these circumstances, it is fair to say that now, more than ever before, police officers in the field, as well as police administrators, need to give greater attention to both the legal and tactical aspects of stop and frisk. (Indeed, greater public awareness would also be beneficial.) To those ends, I recommend this useful work by Doug Mitchell and Greg Connor, which provides extremely valuable information about when and how a stop and frisk ought to be undertaken.

Wayne R. LaFave
David C. Baum Professor Emeritus of Law
and Center for Advanced Study Professor
Emeritus, University of Illinois

Preface

On October 31, 1963, Detective Martin McFadden of the Cleveland (Ohio) Police was on a plainclothes foot patrol assignment in downtown Cleveland. His observations, decisions, and actions that day would eventually be considered by our highest court and have long-term impacts in society, both in and out of law enforcement, that are still important and still developing today.

About 2:30 that afternoon, his attention was drawn to two men, later identified to be John Terry and Richard Chilton. He was unable to explain what made him notice the men, but he decided to watch them. By that time, McFadden had been a police officer for 39 years, the last 30 of which he had been a detective assigned to that area of Cleveland to seek shoplifters and pickpockets. By any definition, that level of experience is likely to have made him an expert in such matters.

Despite not being able to describe at the time what did not look right to him, he followed up on his concern and invested some number of minutes in observing the men in an effort to satisfy his curiosity. Det. McFadden often observed people in that area during his workday. As a result of their actions as he watched them, McFadden concluded that the two men (and a third) were preparing to do a robbery. Not only did he believe it was his duty to investigate further, but he also logically feared that they would have a firearm.

McFadden would make contact, attempt to learn more from the men, and then take physical control of them and pat down their outer clothing. Upon finding firearms concealed on their bodies as a result of this patdown, McFadden arrested them for violating Ohio's prohibition on carrying concealed firearms. A motion to suppress the evidence (the firearms) would be filed, and the trial court would rule in a manner that foreshadowed the Supreme Court's decision in *Terry v. Ohio*, 392 U.S. 1 (1968).

The opinion in the *Terry* case is one of the most important in the Court's treatment of contemporary law enforcement activity. Portions of the analysis and discussion of the case showed the direction in which Fourth Amendment jurisprudence would evolve over the subsequent decades and has remained a focus for function far into the future.

The Court acknowledged that there were significant conflicts between the police and the public they served as a result of this activity. There were, and remain today, strong differences of opinion between law enforcement and some portions of the communities we serve in regard to the legitimacy and basis for the investigative stop. When the second edition of this book was being written, this social tension was again gaining in prominence, with society being forced to face the issues and ideals in conflict. Now, a decade later, the conflict is far greater. The ripples of this conflict of views have spread, resulting in protests and in some cases criminal violence. There are loud voices questioning our actions and, to an unfortunate extent, the law enforcement profession has not helped itself.

The authors still, and even more strongly, believe that unless our profession takes appropriate action to address the developing conflict and improve performance in both enforcement activities and our communication about them, public support and legal justification may needlessly erode or be eliminated. By understanding and applying the legal guidelines addressing this enforcement activity, and the deployment of sound tactical procedures, officers can continue to protect the rights of citizens who may be suspected of criminal activity and simultaneously secure enhanced safety for both themselves and the potential victims of various crimes. This text is designed to address both the legal and procedural aspects inherent in the effort to conduct "objectively reasonable" investigative stops, critical to what surely is a shared goal of societal safety under the rule of law.

Obviously, this text is not a legal treatise designed to answer all of the questions for all of the circumstances of officer/citizen confrontations. One of the treatises reviewed and cited in this text is six volumes and thousands of pages. It is a great resource for the needs of some attorneys but not a practical response to the needs of other members of the community, including law enforcement officers. This text is an effort to blend law and technique into effective tools and tactics and communicate the result to those who need and value this knowledge.

Our goal is that this text will fulfill a variety of training functions for law enforcement. We believe it can be used as part of teaching (a) recruit officers those fundamentals they will need as they begin their professional education, (b) street officers who are practicing aggressive enforcement, (c) Field Training Officers whose duty is to be a resource for on-going enhancement of the enforcement effort, (d) first-line supervisors who need to assess and guide the performance of those they lead, and (e) police managers whose duty is to research, draft, and implement policy that enhances performance. The reporting and recording suggestions of this text are directed to those needs, as the profession as a whole, and most if not virtually all agencies, are operating without useful data to improve their understanding of what is actually being done and what is actually effective.

In addition, the text will help address the communication gap between police legal advisors and their client agencies, as too many times the "language" of the two is not compatible. These advisors must guide agencies in the nuances of the legal aspects of police operations. However, this can be a foreign field to academically trained lawyers. Issues may be vital to the client, even literally life and death, yet are far too often not well understood by the advisor. Similarly, this text can assist in improving criminal prosecutors' ability to understand how they must apply and communicate the wisdom of experienced officers to their litigation role. The authors have been fortunate enough to work in settings in which the vital "cross-pollination" between officers and these attorneys has been valued and performed, but not everyone is. We want to help overcome that gap. We are aware that attempting to address these diverse needs makes parts of the text less approachable for one group or another. We have struggled with the need to provide material in a way that allows peace officers of various ranks to rely upon it, while also providing citations that help the attorneys understand our reasoning and develop their own work from it.

It is also hoped that the research, tactics, and ideas expressed will act as a catalyst to stimulate even greater concern and comprehension of this critical component of the interaction between officers and the individuals they police. The conflict described above is causing new demands to be placed on law enforcement. We must have a substantial improvement in both our performance in the community and our communication about the legitimacy of the actions we take. Some of these legitimate duties are not "people pleasing" but involve coercion that is guided and recognized by the law. Because as a profession we have done a very poor job of communicating this legitimacy, our duties and actions are not just misunderstood. Many believe, and this has been repeated loudly by the media, that our actions are not legitimate and honorable. This is neither based in fact nor tolerable.

In addition to the friction between law enforcement agencies and the communities that they serve, another damaging effect emerges. The very people most in need of our assistance in protecting themselves and their property from criminal actors do not receive that assistance. One of the important duties of law enforcement is to seek out criminals and develop evidence of their conduct. This duty is much more difficult and may become in effect impossible when a significant portion of the impacted community does not support our enforcement efforts due to misperceptions and disinformation. Law enforcement must be "of" not "over" the community. We need to communicate who we are and what we do to all of those residents who should be able to rely on and believe us. When we take the time to educate and develop professional relationships with those who will otherwise question our presence and actions, we overcome the friction and resulting mutual frustration, and thus the reduced crime suppression effectiveness. The potentially positive outcome, not the popular misconception, is the true essence of real community policing.

Acknowledgments

The authors gratefully acknowledge the valuable assistance of the following people, who contributed so much to the creation and evolution of this text:

WAYNE R. LaFAVE, David C. Baum Professor Emeritus of Law and Center for Advanced Study Professor Emeritus, University of Illinois. His review, insight, and guidance cheerfully provided were valuable beyond measure.

SERGEANT ERICK W. GELHAUS, Sonoma County Sheriff's Office, for his effort freely given to review and advise on this text, applying his broad experience and professionalism to help us make sure our thoughts were sound and our expression clear.

PAM CHESTER AND EVE STRILLACCI at Taylor and Francis, who not only tolerated us but helped us navigate the strange new world of publishing.

LT. COL. DAVID BOLGIANO, USAF (Ret.), whose use of some of our preliminary materials resulted in him introducing us to Pam Chester and starting this phase of our work.

JOHN EDWARDS, Executive Director, Peace Officer Association of Georgia Foundation

J. DALE MANN, Georgia Law Enforcement Command College

The unnamed reviewers who provided their thoughts to our editor and confirmed the value of our efforts

Section I

Legal Legacy and Contemporary Update

1   Foundational Concepts

For decades, law enforcement has been moving toward practicality and purpose in its design and delivery. Not unlike the information accumulated over the years in the legal realm, certain control strategies and tactics have evolved that have stood the test of time, proven their value and validity, and have emerged as essential to the safety of officers and suspects alike. A few of these fundamental policing principles are noted below in the interest of ensuring we are all looking at control of encounters in a similar manner.

We hope to have continued to enhance law enforcement performance via this text with the inclusion of various concepts and graphics created to demonstrate maximized safety and performance.

Legal and physical survival for police officers depends on their ability to perceive, assess, and respond to increasing professional challenges. "Terry stops" have great potential to result in conflict between officers and citizens, especially if the necessary legal and tactical fundamentals are neglected. However, they have also been judicially recognized as a valuable means of suppressing and investigating crime.

Foundations of Law Enforcement Activity

The foundation of any law enforcement activity consists of four critical components: **law**, **philosophy**, **strategy**, and **tactics**. Each component is obvious by itself, but it is the integration of them that makes for a completed picture of performance. It is a tapestry, which is a completed work only when all of the threads are present in their proper place.

The **law** is the source of all law enforcement authority: its nature, extent, and limits. These attributes come from constitutions, statutes, and case law, both state and federal. Case law is judicial interpretation and application of those constitutions and statutes to the facts of a specific case. As officers, the law is what makes us different from our fellow citizens within the interactive context of our professional life. The laws we enforce, and our authority to enforce them, generally come from state and local regulatory bodies. The principle source for the limitations of our actions is federal constitutional law. This is because an investigative stop is a "seizure," and as such must be conducted within the Fourth Amendment's limits.

The Fourth Amendment to the U.S. Constitution reads:

> The right of the people to be secure in their persons, houses, papers, and effects, against unreasonable searches and seizures, shall not be violated, and no Warrants shall issue, but upon probable cause, supported by Oath or affirmation and particularly describing the place to be searched, and the persons or things to be seized.

The restrictions placed upon government actions by the Fourth Amendment are the minimum restrictions. There may also be more restrictive provisions in state constitutions and statutes. Although many of these restrictions make our job more difficult, we must all remember that this is not an accident. If one recalls basic government and civics classes, it was a conscious design decision of those who drafted the Constitution and the Bill of Rights, of which the Fourth Amendment is a part. The history of our country, and of England before the American Revolution, included oppressive enforcement activities. The founders of the United States wanted to ensure that such practices would not return.

Obviously, a major emphasis of our text has been the legal basis for our enforcement actions; the ability to conduct a "Terry stop" as we know it today exists in large part due to court cases, the first and most important of which is of course *Terry v. Ohio*, 392 U.S. 1 (1968). Having proceeded through the legal foundation, we now integrate tactical materials in such a manner as to clearly show the interaction of enforcement authority and its implementation.

The *Terry* case is vitally important. The fact that an enforcement activity is known by the name of a United States Supreme Court case tells us of the importance of the case. We have provided a copy of the case after this chapter and recommend that it should be read and reread frequently. However, please remember that the purpose of our text is not to provide a definitive legal analysis of all the implications of *Terry*. The most recent (2012) edition of a leading legal scholar's treatise on the Fourth Amendment has five volumes and an index volume, and with the October 2016 pocket part (updates) dedicates 761 pages to "Stop and Frisk and other lesser intrusions"! We clearly cannot try to replicate that level of knowledge and detail and still have our material be useful to our target audience. That treatise is intended for a very different audience. In doing so, we can only touch upon the high points of constitutional analysis, generally relying only on U.S. Supreme Court cases. By pointing out some of the areas of importance and concern, we hope to stimulate internal research and development within agencies, training academies, and other entities that can and should be among the resources available to law enforcement.

Likewise, we cannot replicate the level of knowledge shown in Urey W. Patrick and John C. Hall, *In Defense of Self and Others—Issues, Facts & Fallacies: The Realities of Law Enforcement's Use of Deadly Force* (3rd edition, 2017), a text that should be possessed and read by anyone with an interest in the topic of law enforcement use of force.

It is possible to demonstrate the hierarchy of the basis for law enforcement actions and the corresponding levels of intrusion. There is a progression from a citizen contact, to an investigative detention, to probable cause to make an arrest. The investigative detention, or "Terry stop," falls into the middle area of intrusion, where perceptions and definitions are imprecise and the difficulty of decision making is most pronounced.

Subsequent chapters will then address increasing levels of intrusion into the actions of citizens, as shown in Figure 1.1, the **Intrusion Chart**. These chapters will continue to build the foundation for your successful use of your lawful authority to conduct investigations of suspicious persons.

One definition of **philosophy** is "the system of values by which one lives"—that is, why we do what we do. Philosophy as used here is not only personal, but it includes department and community philosophy as well, to the extent that those are consistent with our professional obligations.

Strategy and **Tactics** refers to the manner in which we implement our authority. They are the means by which our theoretical ability to engage in an enforcement action becomes operational. They are also the procedures by which we maintain control over our professional obligations.

It has been stated that our most important role is that of a peacekeeper, safeguarding individuals and society from predators. To the extent that this

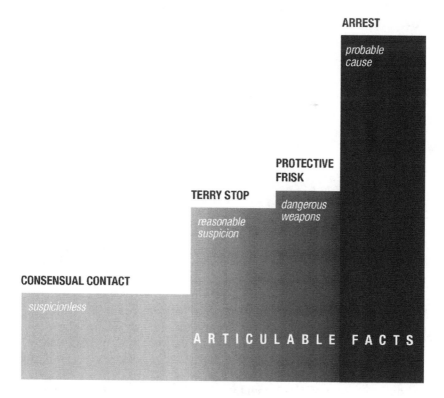

Figure 1.1 Intrusion Chart

describes the greatest extent of our authority and/or responsibility, it is correct. We must seek out and resolve conflicts by whatever means are reasonably necessary. The means by which we accomplish such a goal must possess a reasonable balance in form and force. We have attempted to provide a training foundation "from" the police as well as "for" them. Abuse of police power is a threat to all members of society, and the few officers who engage in improper acts are a menace to the rest of the profession. The safe, effective deployment of the "Terry stop" is one of the most useful tools officers can utilize to protect us all from the criminal element seeking another target for victimization.

The S.E.T. Principle

By dictionary definition, a principle is "a basic quality determining the nature of an activity." The nature of this activity (function) must be a designed, directed, and delivered effort (focus), built upon a "principle-based" sequence. In other words, the foundation of our efforts must be solidly supported by principles that have gained and maintained performance reliability and validity.

Perhaps the most important principle can be best expressed by the acronym **S.E.T.**

> **S:** Safety for the officers and citizens during the enforcement encounter.
> **E:** Effectiveness of the interaction between officers and citizens during this contact experience.
> **T:** Transition potential available for the officer's response to the degree of perceived citizen compliance/noncompliance or other changes in circumstances.

Safety

Remember: no arrest is worth dying for. We feel that the positive performance of enforcement activities is best achieved by utilization of sound, legally validated procedures, based upon a system of strategies and tactics.

Strategy and tactics must be the foundation for our functions while implementing our legal authority during a "Terry stop." The objective of strategy is to diminish the potential for subject noncompliance, with tactics providing the planned basis for the interaction.

In fact, we encourage deployment of what we refer to as the **Encounter Formula** whenever officer and individual contact occurs. The Encounter Formula demands that the officer must presume a *recognized position of advantage* while keeping the subject in a *recognized position of disadvantage*. In this manner the subject's inclination as well as ability to engage in non-compliant actions may be thwarted. In fact, we are simply making use of human risk aversion, by creating a sufficient level of risk or discomfort to discourage non-compliant behavior.

The importance of creating and maintaining a tactical advantage cannot be overstated. Various studies, both within law enforcement agencies and in more academic settings, indicate that many violent conflicts are foreseeable and that bad tactics result from and lead to bad decision making, evolving into bad or even worse outcomes. It is far better to prevent resistance by making it more difficult and less appealing than it is to have to overcome it by the application of force. Sun Tzu told us centuries ago that "to win without fighting is best." However, if despite our positioning and other tactics, resistive or assaultive behavior occurs, we should be in a superior position to control it due to our tactical advantage.

Several elements of encounter have a principle-based tactical expression throughout this text, including:

1. **The utilization of undetected movement and the success associated with surprise**—A confrontational encounter based upon an element of surprise may lead to the even greater potential for discovery and control.
2. **The concept that getting closer to an object or individual may not always be better or safer**—Distancing oneself from the subject or situation can significantly reduce the presentation of a mutually threatening encounter. The selection of cover presupposes that the officer's proximity will establish or even enhance the protective basis.
3. **Don't go to them, direct them to you**—The subject or the situation may be perceived as threatening from the point of initiation. By giving yourself more time to recognize and respond to risk, you enhance your safety. The officer's restraint in terms of immediacy must be conditionally concluded.
4. **Knowing your enforcement environment (lights, structures, locations, etc.) can enhance the Encounter Formula**—Your familiarization with the surroundings and assessed knowledge of the people and things based upon professional familiarity can be crucial in establishing a protective posture and rational response.
5. **"What is done well is done quickly enough"**—The length of an officer and individual's interaction can increase tension and decrease cooperation. Police efficacy includes efficiency and comprehensiveness.

Effectiveness

Each of the safety strategies and tactical procedures presented throughout the text are a result of years of experience and on-going field research seeking to secure maximized safety and efficiency. These tools and tactics were selected based upon their ability to facilitate function and enhance effectiveness.

Transition

This element includes the ability to continually assess the circumstances in any officer/citizen interaction, perceive the degree of subject compliance and/ or noncompliance, assess that and other risks, and then initiate and complete the appropriate reasonable response. As stated by the Arizona Supreme Court, "police interactions with members of the public are inherently fluid, and what begins as a consensual encounter can evolve into a seizure that prompts Fourth Amendment scrutiny." *State v. Serna*, 235 Ariz. 270, 272 331 P. 3d 405 (2014). The principle of transition reflects the U.S. Supreme Court decision in *Graham v. Connor*, 490 U.S. 386 (1989), which suggested the integration of three elements critical to the process of decision making in the determination of "objectively reasonable" force utilization. If this can be perceived by the judiciary, who do not have to apply it in their daily activities, it should be readily apparent to law enforcement officers.

For years, police officers and their agencies have been frustrated by their inability to rapidly respond with competency and confidence in the control of a compliant individual who becomes non-compliant. However, now, by blending the tradition of the ancient martial arts and contemporary police tactics, we have evolved an innovative and flexible control methodology.

For centuries, the Aikido form *Sankyo* has a procedure that practitioners have "gone to" in order to gain subject control. However, in an evolutionary approach the contemporary peace officer can "come from" *Sankyo*, using its potential power toward not only the prevention of non-compliance but, if unsuccessful in its preventative form, to initiate its controlling capability via positional tension. This "adaptive" attribute allows the tactic to be utilized in a variety of applications found throughout enforcement encounters.

At the initiation of physical control, it should start as both a point of domination by the officer and painless to the subject, but with the ability to transition to increase the pain compliance as mandated by the evolving aspects of the interaction based upon the subject's degree of compliance/non-compliance.

Policing is an occupation entirely dependent on individual perception and analysis. Through their training and experience, peace officers should gain both elements. These functional facets may include the gamut from preventative positioning, handcuffing, and even more assertive controls upon non-compliant behavior. Each aspect of the interaction can be initiated from the onset of the officer's tactile connection. These fundamentals are demonstrated in Figure 1.2, the Totality Triangle.

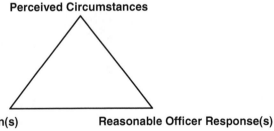

Figure 1.2 Totality Triangle

The **Totality Triangle** depicts the three elements that must be considered in determining whether an application of force was objectively reasonable. It is a means of explaining the application of *Graham v. Connor.*

> **Perceived Circumstances**—the officer's perception of the severity of any crime, the existence of an immediate safety threat to the officer or others, etc.
>
> **Perceived Subject Action(s)**—the subject action(s) as assessed by the reasonable officer
>
> **Reasonable Officer Response(s)**—the reasonable response(s) selected by the officer

Phases of Response Activity

When placed into an encounter, the officer must expand his/her perspective from the common notion of "reaction" into more strategic conduct of an action-initiated **response**. This response should be **proactive**, drawn upon the expertise and experience with the actual subject and situations or other sources of knowledge pertaining to the same or similar participants and incidents. **One need not and should not wait until they have actually been attacked to impose control on the subject.**

Obviously, the officer should remain free of the temptation to pre-judge the subject's actions, and gain the enhanced ability to more properly perceive the **potential** or **actual** actions of the subject in question. Those perceptions must be well communicated as part of the subsequent documentation of the contact.

Strategically, the officer should practice direct, proactive communication toward the individual in an attempt to prevent potential non-compliant behavior within the confrontation. Or, if a conflict is perceived as inevitable, the officer should initiate procedures to provide sufficient systems (strategic planning, distancing, team tactics, etc.) to maximize the safety of him or herself, other officers, and the uninvolved citizens who may be exposed to the consequences of the conflict.

The response must be **active**, in that the controlling tactics the officer initiates will accomplish the control of the subject with a high degree of effectiveness and safety to the officer and to others. In this manner, the confrontation can be controlled as efficiently as possible, thus avoiding the need to resort to higher levels of force with the inherent risks of greater potential injury to the officer, the subject, or others.

And finally, the response must be effective, based on application of lessons learned or researched validity. Most confrontations are not unique or isolated in time; their components will re-occur at other times with other subjects. If a safe, successful solution evolves, the officer should follow that course of response in the future. If the attempted solution is not successful, the officer should use the past experience as a catalyst to seek a safe, effective future solution.

Principle-based safety can only be maintained if officers strategically and systematically anticipate, assess, and act within the effective and accepted parameters of the situation. Officers must understand that this process exists in an environment that is ever changing in definition, direction, depth, and dynamics.

2 Terry v. Ohio

United States Supreme Court
Terry v. Ohio (1968)
No. 67
Argued: December 12, 1967   **Decided: June 10, 1968**

A Cleveland detective (McFadden), on a downtown beat which he had been patrolling for many years, observed two strangers (petitioner and another man, Chilton) on a street corner. He saw them proceed alternately back and forth along an identical route, pausing to stare in the same store window, which they did for a total of about 24 times. Each completion of the route was followed by a conference between the two on a corner, at one of which they were joined by a third man (Katz) who left swiftly. Suspecting the two men of "casing a job, a stick-up," the officer followed them and saw them rejoin the third man a couple of blocks away in front of a store. The officer approached the three, identified himself as a policeman, and asked their names. The men "mumbled something," whereupon McFadden spun petitioner around, patted down his outside clothing, and found in his overcoat pocket, but was unable to remove, a pistol. The officer ordered the three into the store. He removed petitioner's overcoat, took out a revolver, and ordered the three to face the wall with their hands raised. He patted down the outer clothing of Chilton and Katz and seized a revolver from Chilton's outside overcoat pocket. He did not put his hands under the outer garments of Katz (since he discovered nothing in his pat-down which might have been a weapon), or under petitioner's or Chilton's outer garments until he felt the guns. The three were taken to the police station. Petitioner and Chilton were charged with carrying [392 U.S. 1, 2] concealed weapons. The defense moved to suppress the weapons. Though the trial court rejected the prosecution theory that the guns had been seized during a search incident to a lawful arrest, the court denied the motion to suppress and admitted the weapons into evidence on the ground that the officer had cause to believe that petitioner and Chilton were acting suspiciously, that their interrogation was warranted, and that the officer for his own protection had the right to pat down their outer clothing having reasonable cause to believe that they might be armed. The court distinguished between an investigatory "stop" and an arrest, and between a "frisk" of the outer clothing for weapons and a full-blown search for evidence of crime. Petitioner and Chilton were found guilty, an intermediate appellate court affirmed, and the State Supreme Court dismissed the appeal on the ground that "no substantial constitutional question" was involved. Held:

1. The Fourth Amendment right against unreasonable searches and seizures, made applicable to the States by the Fourteenth Amendment, "protects people, not places," and therefore applies as much to the citizen on the streets as well as at home or elsewhere. Pp. 8–9.
2. The issue in this case is not the abstract propriety of the police conduct but the admissibility against petitioner of the evidence uncovered by the search and seizure. P. 12.
3. The exclusionary rule cannot properly be invoked to exclude the products of legitimate and restrained police investigative techniques; and this Court's approval of such techniques should not discourage remedies other than the exclusionary rule to curtail police abuses for which that is not an effective sanction. Pp. 13–15.
4. The Fourth Amendment applies to "stop and frisk" procedures such as those followed here. Pp. 16–20.

    (a) Whenever a police officer accosts an individual and restrains his freedom to walk away, he has "seized" that person within the meaning of the Fourth Amendment. P. 16.
    (b) A careful exploration of the outer surfaces of a person's clothing in an attempt to find weapons is a "search" under that Amendment. P. 16.

5. Where a reasonably prudent officer is warranted in the circumstances of a given case in believing that his safety or that of others is endangered, he may make a reasonable search for weapons of the person believed by him to be armed and dangerous [392 U.S. 1, 3] regardless of whether he has probable cause to arrest that individual for crime or the absolute certainty that the individual is armed. Pp. 20–27.

    (a) Though the police must whenever practicable secure a warrant to make a search and seizure, that procedure cannot be followed where swift action based upon on-the-spot observations of the officer on the beat is required. P. 20.
    (b) The reasonableness of any particular search and seizure must be assessed in light of the particular circumstances against the standard of whether a man of reasonable caution is warranted in believing that the action taken was appropriate. Pp. 21–22.
    (c) The officer here was performing a legitimate function of investigating suspicious conduct when he decided to approach petitioner and his companions. P. 22.

(d) An officer justified in believing that an individual whose suspicious behavior he is investigating at close range is armed may, to neutralize the threat of physical harm, take necessary measures to determine whether that person is carrying a weapon. P. 24.

(e) A search for weapons in the absence of probable cause to arrest must be strictly circumscribed by the exigencies of the situation. Pp. 25–26.

(f) An officer may make an intrusion short of arrest where he has reasonable apprehension of danger before being possessed of information justifying arrest. Pp. 26–27.

6. The officer's protective seizure of petitioner and his companions and the limited search which he made were reasonable, both at their inception and as conducted. Pp. 27–30.

(a) The actions of petitioner and his companions were consistent with the officer's hypothesis that they were contemplating a daylight robbery and were armed. P. 28.

(b) The officer's search was confined to what was minimally necessary to determine whether the men were armed, and the intrusion, which was made for the sole purpose of protecting himself and others nearby, was confined to ascertaining the presence of weapons. Pp. 29–30.

7. The revolver seized from petitioner was properly admitted into evidence against him, since the search which led to its seizure was reasonable under the Fourth Amendment. Pp. 30–31.

Affirmed. [392 U.S. 1, 4]

Louis Stokes argued the cause for petitioner. With him on the brief was Jack G. Day.

Reuben M. Payne argued the cause for respondent. With him on the brief was John T. Corrigan.

Briefs of amici curiae, urging reversal, were filed by Jack Greenberg, James M. Nabrit III, Michael Meltsner, Melvyn Zarr, and Anthony G. Amsterdam for the NAACP Legal Defense and Educational Fund, Inc., and by Bernard A. Berkman, Melvin L. Wulf, and Alan H. Levine for the American Civil Liberties Union et al.

Briefs of amici curiae, urging affirmance, were filed by Solicitor General Griswold, Assistant Attorney General Vinson, Ralph S. Spritzer, Beatrice Rosenberg, and Mervyn Hamburg for the United States; by Louis J. Lefkowitz, pro se, Samuel A. Hirshowitz, First Assistant Attorney General, and Maria L. Marcus and Brenda Soloff, Assistant Attorneys General, for the Attorney General of New York; by Charles Moylan, Jr., Evelle J. Younger, and Harry Wood for the National District Attorneys' Assn., and by James R. Thompson for Americans for Effective Law Enforcement.

MR. CHIEF JUSTICE WARREN delivered the opinion of the Court.

This case presents serious questions concerning the role of the Fourth Amendment in the confrontation on the street between the citizen and the policeman investigating suspicious circumstances.

Petitioner Terry was convicted of carrying a concealed weapon and sentenced to the statutorily prescribed term of one to three years in the penitentiary.[1] Following [392 U.S. 1, 5] the denial of a pretrial motion to suppress, the prosecution introduced in evidence two revolvers and a number of bullets seized from Terry and a codefendant, Richard Chilton,[2] by Cleveland Police Detective Martin McFadden. At the hearing on the motion to suppress this evidence, Officer McFadden testified that while he was patrolling in plain clothes in downtown Cleveland at approximately 2:30 in the afternoon of October 31, 1963, his attention was attracted by two men, Chilton and Terry, standing on the corner of Huron Road and Euclid Avenue. He had never seen the two men before, and he was unable to say precisely what first drew his eye to them. However, he testified that he had been a policeman for 39 years and a detective for 35 and that he had been assigned to patrol this vicinity of downtown Cleveland for shoplifters and pickpockets for 30 years. He explained that he had developed routine habits of observation over the years and that he would "stand and watch people or walk and watch people at many intervals of the day." He added: "Now, in this case when I looked over they didn't look right to me at the time."

His interest aroused, Officer McFadden took up a post of observation in the entrance to a store 300 to 400 feet [392 U.S. 1, 6] away from the two men. "I get more purpose to watch them when I seen their movements," he testified. He saw one of the men leave the other one and walk southwest on Huron Road, past some stores. The man paused for a moment and looked in a store window, then walked on a short distance, turned around and walked back toward the corner, pausing once again to look in the same store window. He rejoined his companion at the corner, and the two conferred briefly. Then the second man went through the same series of motions, strolling down Huron Road, looking in the same window, walking on a short distance, turning back, peering in the store window again, and returning to confer with the first man at the corner. The two men repeated this ritual alternately between five and six times apiece—in all, roughly a dozen trips. At one point, while the two were standing together on the corner, a third man approached them and engaged them briefly in conversation. This man then left the two others and walked west on Euclid Avenue. Chilton and Terry resumed their measured pacing, peering, and conferring. After this had gone on for 10 to 12 minutes, the two men walked off together, heading west on Euclid Avenue, following the path taken earlier by the third man.

By this time Officer McFadden had become thoroughly suspicious. He testified that after observing their elaborately casual and oft-repeated reconnaissance of the store window on Huron Road, he suspected the two men of "casing a job, a stick-up," and that he considered it his duty as a police officer to investigate further. He added that he feared "they may have a gun." Thus, Officer McFadden followed Chilton and Terry and saw them stop in front of Zucker's store to talk to the same man who had conferred with them earlier on the street corner. Deciding that the situation was ripe for direct action, Officer McFadden approached the three men, identified [392 U.S. 1, 7] himself as a police officer and asked for their names. At this point his knowledge was confined to what he had observed. He was not acquainted with any of the three men by name or by sight, and he had received no information concerning them from any other source. When the men "mumbled something" in response to his inquiries, Officer McFadden grabbed petitioner Terry, spun him around so that they were facing the other two, with Terry between McFadden and the others, and patted down the outside of his clothing. In the left breast pocket of Terry's overcoat Officer McFadden felt a pistol. He reached inside the overcoat pocket, but was unable to remove the gun. At this point, keeping Terry between himself and the others, the officer ordered all three men to enter Zucker's store. As they went in, he removed Terry's overcoat completely, removed a .38-caliber revolver from the pocket and ordered all three men to face the wall with their hands raised. Officer McFadden proceeded to pat down the outer clothing of Chilton and the third man, Katz. He discovered another revolver in the outer pocket of Chilton's overcoat, but no weapons were found on Katz. The officer testified that he only patted the men down to see whether they had weapons, and that he did not put his hands beneath the outer garments of either Terry or Chilton until he felt their guns. So far as appears from the record, he never placed his hands beneath Katz' outer garments. Officer McFadden seized Chilton's gun, asked the proprietor of the store to call a police wagon, and took all three men to the station, where Chilton and Terry were formally charged with carrying concealed weapons.

On the motion to suppress the guns the prosecution took the position that they had been seized following a search incident to a lawful arrest. The trial court rejected this theory, stating that it "would be stretching the facts beyond reasonable comprehension" to find that Officer [392 U.S. 1, 8] McFadden had had probable cause to arrest the men before he patted them down for weapons. However, the court denied the defendants' motion on the ground that Officer McFadden, on the basis of his experience, "had reasonable cause to believe . . . that the defendants were conducting themselves suspiciously, and some interrogation should be made of their action." Purely for his own protection, the court held, the officer had the right to pat down the outer clothing of these men, who he had reasonable cause to believe might be armed. The court distinguished between an investigatory "stop" and an arrest, and between a "frisk" of the outer clothing for weapons and a full-blown search for evidence of crime. The frisk, it held, was essential to the proper performance of the officer's investigatory duties, for without it "the answer to the police officer may be a bullet, and a loaded pistol discovered during the frisk is admissible."

After the court denied their motion to suppress, Chilton and Terry waived jury trial and pleaded not guilty. The court adjudged them guilty, and the Court of Appeals for the Eighth Judicial District, Cuyahoga County, affirmed. State v. Terry, 5 Ohio App. 2d 122, 214 N. E. 2d 114 (1966). The Supreme Court of Ohio dismissed their appeal on the ground that no "substantial constitutional question" was involved. We granted certiorari, 387 U.S. 929 (1967), to determine whether the admission of the revolvers in evidence violated petitioner's rights under the Fourth Amendment, made applicable to the States by the Fourteenth. Mapp v. Ohio, 367 U.S. 643 (1961). We affirm the conviction.

I

The Fourth Amendment provides that "the right of the people to be secure in their persons, houses, papers, and effects, against unreasonable searches and seizures, shall not be violated. . . ." This inestimable right of [392 U.S. 1, 9] personal security belongs as much to the citizen on the streets of our cities as to the homeowner closeted in his study to dispose of his secret affairs. For, as this Court has always recognized, "No right is held more sacred, or is more carefully guarded, by the common law, than the right of every individual to the possession and control of his own person, free from all restraint or interference of others, unless by clear and unquestionable authority of law." Union Pac. R. Co. v. Botsford, 141 U.S. 250, 251 (1891).

We have recently held that "the Fourth Amendment protects people, not places," Katz v. United States, 389 U.S. 347, 351 (1967), and wherever an individual may harbor a reasonable "expectation of privacy," id., at 361 (MR. JUSTICE HARLAN, concurring), he is entitled to be free from unreasonable governmental intrusion. Of course, the specific content and incidents of this right must be shaped by the context in which it is asserted. For "what the Constitution forbids is not all searches and seizures, but unreasonable searches and seizures." Elkins v. United States, 364 U.S. 206, 222 (1960). Unquestionably petitioner was entitled to the protection of the Fourth Amendment as he walked down the street in Cleveland. Beck v. Ohio, 379 U.S. 89 (1964); Rios v. United States, 364 U.S. 253 (1960); Henry v. United States, 361 U.S. 98 (1959); United States v. Di Re, 332 U.S. 581 (1948); Carroll v. United States, 267 U.S. 132 (1925). The question is whether in all the circumstances of this on-the-street encounter, his right to personal security was violated by an unreasonable search and seizure.

We would be less than candid if we did not acknowledge that this question thrusts to the fore difficult and troublesome issues regarding a sensitive area of police activity—issues which have never before been squarely [392 U.S. 1, 10] presented to this Court. Reflective of the tensions involved are the practical and constitutional arguments pressed with great vigor on both sides of the public debate over the power of the police to "stop and frisk"—as it is sometimes euphemistically termed—suspicious persons.

On the one hand, it is frequently argued that in dealing with the rapidly unfolding and often dangerous situations on city streets the police are in need of an escalating set of flexible responses, graduated in relation to the amount of information they possess. For this purpose it is urged that distinctions should be made between a "stop" and an "arrest" (or a "seizure" of a person), and between a "frisk" and a "search."[3] Thus, it is argued, the police should be allowed to "stop" a person and detain him briefly for questioning upon suspicion that he may be connected with criminal activity. Upon suspicion that the person may be armed, the police should have the power to "frisk" him for weapons. If the "stop" and the "frisk" give rise to probable cause to believe that the suspect has committed a crime, then the police should be empowered to make a formal "arrest," and a full incident "search" of the person. This scheme is justified in part upon the notion that a "stop" and a "frisk" amount to a mere "minor inconvenience and petty indignity,"[4] which can properly be imposed upon the [392 U.S. 1, 11] citizen in the interest of effective law enforcement on the basis of a police officer's suspicion.[5]

On the other side the argument is made that the authority of the police must be strictly circumscribed by the law of arrest and search as it has developed to date in the traditional jurisprudence of the Fourth Amendment.[6] It is contended with some force that there is not—and cannot be—a variety of police activity which does not depend solely upon the voluntary cooperation of the citizen and yet which stops short of an arrest based upon probable cause to make such an arrest. The heart of the Fourth Amendment, the argument runs, is a severe requirement of specific justification for any intrusion upon protected personal security, coupled with a highly developed system of judicial controls to enforce upon the agents of the State the commands of the Constitution. Acquiescence by the courts in the compulsion inherent [392 U.S. 1, 12] in the field interrogation practices at issue here, it is urged, would constitute an abdication of judicial control over, and indeed an encouragement of, substantial interference with liberty and personal security by police officers whose judgment is necessarily colored by their primary involvement in "the often competitive enterprise of ferreting out crime." Johnson v. United States, 333 U.S. 10, 14 (1948). This, it is argued, can only serve to exacerbate police-community tensions in the crowded centers of our Nation's cities.[7]

In this context we approach the issues in this case mindful of the limitations of the judicial function in controlling the myriad daily situations in which policemen and citizens confront each other on the street. The State has characterized the issue here as "the right of a police officer . . . to make an on-the-street stop, interrogate and pat down for weapons (known in street vernacular as 'stop and frisk')."[8] But this is only partly accurate. For the issue is not the abstract propriety of the police conduct, but the admissibility against petitioner of the evidence uncovered by the search and seizure. Ever since its inception, the rule excluding evidence seized in violation of the Fourth Amendment has been recognized as a principal mode of discouraging lawless police conduct. See Weeks v. United States, 232 U.S. 383, 391–393 (1914). Thus its major thrust is a deterrent one, see Linkletter v. Walker, 381 U.S. 618, 629–635 (1965), and experience has taught that it is the only effective deterrent to police misconduct in the criminal context, and that without it the constitutional guarantee against unreasonable searches and seizures would be a mere "form of words." Mapp v. Ohio, 367 U.S. 643, 655 (1961). The rule also serves another vital function—"the imperative of judicial integrity." Elkins [392 U.S. 1, 13] v. United States, 364 U.S. 206, 222 (1960). Courts which sit under our Constitution cannot and will not be made party to lawless invasions of the constitutional rights of citizens by permitting unhindered governmental use of the fruits of such invasions. Thus in our system evidentiary rulings provide the context in which the judicial process of inclusion and exclusion approves some conduct as comporting with constitutional guarantees and disapproves other actions by state agents. A ruling admitting evidence in a criminal trial, we recognize, has the necessary effect of legitimizing the conduct which produced the evidence, while an application of the exclusionary rule withholds the constitutional imprimatur.

The exclusionary rule has its limitations, however, as a tool of judicial control. It cannot properly be invoked to exclude the products of legitimate police investigative techniques on the ground that much conduct which is closely similar involves unwarranted intrusions upon constitutional protections. Moreover, in some contexts the rule is ineffective as a deterrent. Street encounters between citizens and police officers are incredibly rich in diversity. They range from wholly friendly exchanges of pleasantries or mutually useful information to hostile confrontations of armed men involving arrests, or injuries, or loss of life. Moreover, hostile confrontations are not all of a piece. Some of them begin in a friendly enough manner, only to take a different turn upon the injection of some unexpected element into the conversation. Encounters are initiated by the police for a wide variety of purposes, some of which are wholly unrelated to a desire to prosecute for crime.[9] Doubtless some [392 U.S. 1, 14] police "field interrogation" conduct violates the Fourth Amendment. But a stern refusal by this Court to condone such activity does not necessarily render it responsive to the exclusionary rule. Regardless of how effective the rule may be where obtaining convictions is an important objective of the police,[10] it is powerless to deter invasions of constitutionally guaranteed rights where the police either have no interest in prosecuting or are willing to forgo successful prosecution in the interest of serving some other goal.

Proper adjudication of cases in which the exclusionary rule is invoked demands a constant awareness of these limitations. The wholesale harassment by certain elements of the police community, of which minority groups, particularly Negroes, frequently complain,[11] will not be [392 U.S. 1, 15] stopped by the exclusion of any evidence from any criminal trial. Yet a rigid and unthinking application of the exclusionary rule, in futile protest against practices which it can never be used effectively to control, may exact a high toll in human injury and frustration of efforts to prevent crime. No judicial opinion can comprehend the protean variety of the street encounter, and we can only judge the facts of the case before us. Nothing we say today is to be taken as indicating approval of police conduct outside the legitimate investigative sphere. Under our decision, courts still retain their traditional responsibility to guard against police conduct which is overbearing or harassing, or which trenches upon personal security without the objective evidentiary justification which the Constitution requires. When such conduct is identified, it must be condemned by the judiciary and its fruits must be excluded from evidence in criminal trials. And, of course, our approval of legitimate and restrained investigative conduct undertaken on the basis of ample factual justification should in no way discourage the employment of other remedies than the exclusionary rule to curtail abuses for which that sanction may prove inappropriate.

Having thus roughly sketched the perimeters of the constitutional debate over the limits on police investigative conduct in general and the background against which this case presents itself, we turn our attention to the quite narrow question posed by the facts before us: whether it is always unreasonable for a policeman to seize a person and subject him to a limited search for weapons unless there is probable cause for an arrest. [392 U.S. 1, 16] Given the narrowness of this question, we have no occasion to canvass in detail the constitutional limitations upon the scope of a policeman's power when he confronts a citizen without probable cause to arrest him.

II

Our first task is to establish at what point in this encounter the Fourth Amendment becomes relevant. That is, we must decide whether and when Officer McFadden "seized" Terry and whether and when he conducted a "search." There is some suggestion in the use of such terms as "stop" and "frisk" that such police conduct is outside the purview of the Fourth Amendment because neither action rises to the level of a "search" or "seizure" within the meaning of the Constitution.[12] We emphatically reject this notion. It is quite plain that the Fourth Amendment governs "seizures" of the person which do not eventuate in a trip to the station house and prosecution for crime—"arrests" in traditional terminology. It must be recognized that whenever a police officer accosts an individual and restrains his freedom to walk away, he has "seized" that person. And it is nothing less than sheer torture of the English language to suggest that a careful exploration of the outer surfaces of a person's clothing all over his or her body in an attempt to find weapons is not a "search." Moreover, it is simply fantastic to urge that such a procedure [392 U.S. 1, 17] performed in public by a policeman while the citizen stands helpless, perhaps facing a wall with his hands raised, is a "petty indignity."[13] It is a serious intrusion upon the sanctity of the person, which may inflict great indignity and arouse strong resentment, and it is not to be undertaken lightly.[14]

The danger in the logic which proceeds upon distinctions between a "stop" and an "arrest," or "seizure" of the person, and between a "frisk" and a "search" is two-fold. It seeks to isolate from constitutional scrutiny the initial stages of the contact between the policeman and the citizen. And by suggesting a rigid all-or-nothing model of justification and regulation under the Amendment, it obscures the utility of limitations upon the scope, as well as the initiation, of police action as a means of constitutional regulation.[15] This Court has held in [392 U.S. 1, 18] the past that a search which is reasonable at its inception may violate the Fourth Amendment by virtue of its intolerable intensity and scope. Kremen v. United States, 353 U.S. 346 (1957); Go-Bart Importing Co. v. [392 U.S. 1, 19] United States, 282 U.S. 344, 356–358 (1931); see United States v. Di Re, 332 U.S. 581, 586–587 (1948). The scope of the search must be "strictly tied to and justified by" the circumstances which rendered its initiation permissible. Warden v. Hayden, 387 U.S. 294, 310 (1967) (MR. JUSTICE FORTAS, concurring); see, e.g., Preston v. United States, 376 U.S. 364, 367–368 (1964); Agnello v. United States, 269 U.S. 20, 30–31 (1925).

The distinctions of classical "stop and frisk" theory thus serve to divert attention from the central inquiry under the Fourth Amendment—the reasonableness in all the circumstances of the particular governmental invasion of a citizen's personal security. "Search" and "seizure" are not talismans. We therefore reject the notions that the Fourth Amendment does not come into play at all as a limitation upon police conduct if the officers stop short of something called a "technical arrest" or a "full-blown search."

In this case there can be no question, then, that Officer McFadden "seized" petitioner and subjected him to a "search" when he took hold of him and patted down the outer surfaces of his clothing. We must decide whether at that point it was reasonable for Officer McFadden to have interfered with petitioner's personal security as he did.[16] And in determining whether the seizure and search were "unreasonable" our inquiry [392 U.S. 1, 20] is a dual one—whether the officer's action was justified at its inception, and whether it was reasonably related in scope to the circumstances which justified the interference in the first place.

III

If this case involved police conduct subject to the Warrant Clause of the Fourth Amendment, we would have to ascertain whether "probable cause" existed to justify the search and seizure which took place. However, that is not the case. We do not retreat from our holdings that the police must, whenever practicable, obtain advance judicial approval of searches and seizures through the warrant procedure, see, e.g., Katz v. United States, 389 U.S. 347 (1967); Beck v. Ohio, 379 U.S. 89, 96 (1964); Chapman v. United States, 365 U.S. 610 (1961), or that in most instances failure to comply with the warrant requirement can only be excused by exigent circumstances, see, e.g., Warden v. Hayden, 387 U.S. 294 (1967) (hot pursuit); cf. Preston v. United States, 376 U.S. 364, 367–368 (1964). But we deal here with an entire rubric of police conduct—necessarily swift action predicated upon the on-the-spot observations of the officer on the beat—which historically has not been, and as a practical matter could not be, subjected to the warrant procedure. Instead, the conduct involved in this case must be tested by the Fourth Amendment's general proscription against unreasonable searches and seizures.[17]

Nonetheless, the notions which underlie both the warrant procedure and the requirement of probable cause remain fully relevant in this context. In order to assess the reasonableness of Officer McFadden's conduct as a general proposition, it is necessary "first to focus upon [392 U.S. 1, 21] the governmental interest which allegedly justifies official intrusion upon the constitutionally protected interests of the private citizen," for there is "no ready test for determining reasonableness other than by balancing the need to search [or seize] against the invasion which the search [or seizure] entails." Camara v. Municipal Court, 387 U.S. 523, 534–535, 536–537 (1967). And in justifying the particular intrusion the police officer must be able to point to specific and articulable facts which, taken together with rational inferences from those facts, reasonably warrant that intrusion.[18] The scheme of the Fourth Amendment becomes meaningful only when it is assured that at some point the conduct of those charged with enforcing the laws can be subjected to the more detached, neutral scrutiny of a judge who must evaluate the reasonableness of a particular search or seizure in light of the particular circumstances.[19] And in making that assessment it is imperative that the facts be judged against an objective standard: would the facts [392 U.S. 1, 22] available to the officer at the moment of the seizure or the search "warrant a man of reasonable caution in the belief" that the action taken was appropriate? Cf. Carroll v. United States, 267 U.S. 132 (1925); Beck v. Ohio, 379 U.S. 89, 96–97 (1964).[20] Anything less would invite intrusions upon constitutionally guaranteed rights based on nothing more substantial than inarticulate hunches, a result this Court has consistently refused to sanction. See, e.g., Beck v. Ohio, supra; Rios v. United States, 364 U.S. 253 (1960); Henry v. United States, 361 U.S. 98 (1959). And simple "'good faith on the part of the arresting officer is not enough.' . . . If subjective good faith alone were the test, the protections of the Fourth Amendment would evaporate, and the people would be 'secure in their persons, houses, papers, and effects,' only in the discretion of the police." Beck v. Ohio, supra, at 97.

Applying these principles to this case, we consider first the nature and extent of the governmental interests involved. One general interest is of course that of effective crime prevention and detection; it is this interest which underlies the recognition that a police officer may in appropriate circumstances and in an appropriate manner approach a person for purposes of investigating possibly criminal behavior even though there is no probable cause to make an arrest. It was this legitimate investigative function Officer McFadden was discharging when he decided to approach petitioner and his companions. He had observed Terry, Chilton, and Katz go through a series of acts, each of them perhaps innocent in itself, but which taken together warranted further investigation. There is nothing unusual in two men standing together on a street corner, perhaps waiting for someone. Nor is there anything suspicious about people [392 U.S. 1, 23] in such circumstances strolling up and down the street, singly or in pairs. Store windows, moreover, are made to be looked in. But the story is quite different where, as here, two men hover about a street corner for an extended period of time, at the end of which it becomes apparent that they are not waiting for anyone or anything; where these men pace alternately along an identical route, pausing to stare in the same store window roughly 24 times; where each completion of this route is followed immediately by a conference between the two men on the corner; where they are joined in one of these conferences by a third man who leaves swiftly; and where the two men finally follow the third and rejoin him a couple of blocks away. It would have been poor police work indeed for an officer of 30 years' experience in the detection of thievery from stores in this same neighborhood to have failed to investigate this behavior further.

The crux of this case, however, is not the propriety of Officer McFadden's taking steps to investigate petitioner's suspicious behavior, but rather, whether there was justification for McFadden's invasion of Terry's personal security by searching him for weapons in the course of that investigation. We are now concerned with more than the governmental interest in investigating crime; in addition, there is the more immediate interest of the police officer in taking steps to assure himself that the person with whom he is dealing is not armed with a weapon that could unexpectedly and fatally be used against him. Certainly it would be unreasonable to require that police officers take unnecessary risks in the performance of their duties. American criminals have a long tradition of armed violence, and every year in this country many law enforcement officers are killed in the line of duty, and thousands more are wounded. [392 U.S. 1, 24] Virtually all of these deaths and a substantial portion of the injuries are inflicted with guns and knives.[21]

In view of these facts, we cannot blind ourselves to the need for law enforcement officers to protect themselves and other prospective victims of violence in situations where they may lack probable cause for an arrest. When an officer is justified in believing that the individual whose suspicious behavior he is investigating at close range is armed and presently dangerous to the officer or to others, it would appear to be clearly unreasonable to deny the officer the power to take necessary measures to determine whether the person is in fact carrying a weapon and to neutralize the threat of physical harm.

We must still consider, however, the nature and quality of the intrusion on individual rights which must be accepted if police officers are to be conceded the right to search for weapons in situations where probable cause to arrest for crime is lacking. Even a limited search of the outer clothing for weapons constitutes a severe, [392 U.S. 1, 25] though brief, intrusion upon cherished personal security, and it must surely be an annoying, frightening, and perhaps humiliating experience. Petitioner contends that such an intrusion is permissible only incident to a lawful arrest, either for a crime involving the possession of weapons or for a crime the commission of which led the officer to investigate in the first place. However, this argument must be closely examined.

Petitioner does not argue that a police officer should refrain from making any investigation of suspicious circumstances until such time as he has probable cause to make an arrest; nor does he deny that police officers in properly discharging their investigative function may find themselves confronting persons who might well be armed and dangerous. Moreover, he does not say that an officer is always unjustified in searching a suspect to discover weapons. Rather, he says it is unreasonable for the policeman to take that step until such time as the situation evolves to a point where there is probable cause to make an arrest. When that point has been reached, petitioner would concede the officer's right to conduct a search of the suspect for weapons, fruits or instrumentalities of the crime, or "mere" evidence, incident to the arrest.

There are two weaknesses in this line of reasoning, however. First, it fails to take account of traditional limitations upon the scope of searches, and thus recognizes no distinction in purpose, character, and extent between a search incident to an arrest and a limited search for weapons. The former, although justified in part by the acknowledged necessity to protect the arresting officer from assault with a concealed weapon, Preston v. United States, 376 U.S. 364, 367 (1964), is also justified on other grounds, ibid., and can therefore involve a relatively extensive exploration of the person. A search for weapons in the absence of probable cause to [392 U.S. 1, 26] arrest, however, must, like any other search, be strictly circumscribed by the exigencies which justify its initiation. Warden v. Hayden, 387 U.S. 294, 310 (1967) (MR. JUSTICE FORTAS, concurring). Thus it must be limited to that which is necessary for the discovery of weapons which might be used to harm the officer or others nearby, and may realistically be characterized as something less than a "full" search, even though it remains a serious intrusion.

A second, and related, objection to petitioner's argument is that it assumes that the law of arrest has already worked out the balance between the particular interests involved here—the neutralization of danger to the policeman in the investigative circumstance and the sanctity of the individual. But this is not so. An arrest is a wholly different kind of intrusion upon individual freedom from a limited search for weapons, and the interests each is designed to serve are likewise quite different. An arrest is the initial stage of a criminal prosecution. It is intended to vindicate society's interest in having its laws obeyed, and it is inevitably accompanied by future interference with the individual's freedom of movement, whether or not trial or conviction ultimately follows.[22] The protective search for weapons, on the other hand, constitutes a brief, though far from inconsiderable, intrusion upon the sanctity of the person. It does not follow that because an officer may lawfully arrest a person only when he is apprised of facts sufficient to warrant a belief that the person has committed or is committing a crime, the officer is equally unjustified, absent that kind of evidence, in making any intrusions short of an arrest. Moreover, a perfectly reasonable apprehension of danger may arise long before the officer is possessed of adequate information to justify taking a person into custody for [392 U.S. 1, 27] the purpose of prosecuting him for a crime. Petitioner's reliance on cases which have worked out standards of reasonableness with regard to "seizures" constituting arrests and searches incident thereto is thus misplaced. It assumes that the interests sought to be vindicated and the invasions of personal security may be equated in the two cases, and thereby ignores a vital aspect of the analysis of the reasonableness of particular types of conduct under the Fourth Amendment. See Camara v. Municipal Court, supra.

Our evaluation of the proper balance that has to be struck in this type of case leads us to conclude that there must be a narrowly drawn authority to permit a reasonable search for weapons for the protection of the police officer, where he has reason to believe that he is dealing with an armed and dangerous individual, regardless of whether he has probable cause to arrest the individual for a crime. The officer need not be absolutely certain that the individual is armed; the issue is whether a reasonably prudent man in the circumstances would be warranted in the belief that his safety or that of others was in danger. Cf. Beck v. Ohio, 379 U.S. 89, 91 (1964); Brinegar v. United States, 338 U.S. 160, 174–176 (1949); Stacey v. Emery, 97 U.S. 642, 645 (1878).[23] And in determining whether the officer acted reasonably in such circumstances, due weight must be given, not to his inchoate and unparticularized suspicion or "hunch," but to the specific reasonable inferences which he is entitled to draw from the facts in light of his experience. Cf. Brinegar v. United States, supra.

IV

We must now examine the conduct of Officer McFadden in this case to determine whether his search and seizure of petitioner were reasonable, both at their inception [392 U.S. 1, 28] and as conducted. He had observed Terry, together with Chilton and another man, acting in a manner he took to be preface to a "stick-up." We think on the facts and circumstances Officer McFadden detailed before the trial judge a reasonably prudent man would have been warranted in believing petitioner was armed and thus presented a threat to the officer's safety while he was investigating his suspicious behavior. The actions of Terry and Chilton were consistent with McFadden's hypothesis that these men were contemplating a daylight robbery—which, it is reasonable to assume, would be likely to involve the use of weapons—and nothing in their conduct from the time he first noticed them until the time he confronted them and identified himself as a police officer gave him sufficient reason to negate that hypothesis. Although the trio had departed the original scene, there was nothing to indicate abandonment of an intent to commit a robbery at some point. Thus, when Officer McFadden approached the three men gathered before the display window at Zucker's store he had observed enough to make it quite reasonable to fear that they were armed;

and nothing in their response to his hailing them, identifying himself as a police officer, and asking their names served to dispel that reasonable belief. We cannot say his decision at that point to seize Terry and pat his clothing for weapons was the product of a volatile or inventive imagination, or was undertaken simply as an act of harassment; the record evidences the tempered act of a policeman who in the course of an investigation had to make a quick decision as to how to protect himself and others from possible danger, and took limited steps to do so.

The manner in which the seizure and search were conducted is, of course, as vital a part of the inquiry as whether they were warranted at all. The Fourth Amendment proceeds as much by limitations upon the [392 U.S. 1, 29] scope of governmental action as by imposing preconditions upon its initiation. Compare Katz v. United States, 389 U.S. 347, 354–356 (1967). The entire deterrent purpose of the rule excluding evidence seized in violation of the Fourth Amendment rests on the assumption that "limitations upon the fruit to be gathered tend to limit the quest itself." United States v. Poller, 43 F.2d 911, 914 (C. A. 2d Cir. 1930); see, e.g., Linkletter v. Walker, 381 U.S. 618, 629–635 (1965); Mapp v. Ohio, 367 U.S. 643 (1961); Elkins v. United States, 364 U.S. 206, 216–221 (1960). Thus, evidence may not be introduced if it was discovered by means of a seizure and search which were not reasonably related in scope to the justification for their initiation. Warden v. Hayden, 387 U.S. 294, 310 (1967) (MR. JUSTICE FORTAS, concurring).

We need not develop at length in this case, however, the limitations which the Fourth Amendment places upon a protective seizure and search for weapons. These limitations will have to be developed in the concrete factual circumstances of individual cases. See Sibron v. New York, post, p. 40, decided today. Suffice it to note that such a search, unlike a search without a warrant incident to a lawful arrest, is not justified by any need to prevent the disappearance or destruction of evidence of crime. See Preston v. United States, 376 U.S. 364, 367 (1964). The sole justification of the search in the present situation is the protection of the police officer and others nearby, and it must therefore be confined in scope to an intrusion reasonably designed to discover guns, knives, clubs, or other hidden instruments for the assault of the police officer.

The scope of the search in this case presents no serious problem in light of these standards. Officer McFadden patted down the outer clothing of petitioner and his two companions. He did not place his hands in their pockets or under the outer surface of their garments until he had [392 U.S. 1, 30] felt weapons, and then he merely reached for and removed the guns. He never did invade Katz' person beyond the outer surfaces of his clothes, since he discovered nothing in his patdown which might have been a weapon. Officer McFadden confined his search strictly to what was minimally necessary to learn whether the men were armed and to disarm them once he discovered the weapons. He did not conduct a general exploratory search for whatever evidence of criminal activity he might find.

V

We conclude that the revolver seized from Terry was properly admitted in evidence against him. At the time he seized petitioner and searched him for weapons, Officer McFadden had reasonable grounds to believe that petitioner was armed and dangerous, and it was necessary for the protection of himself and others to take swift measures to discover the true facts and neutralize the threat of harm if it materialized. The policeman carefully restricted his search to what was appropriate to the discovery of the particular items which he sought. Each case of this sort will, of course, have to be decided on its own facts. We merely hold today that where a police officer observes unusual conduct which leads him reasonably to conclude in light of his experience that criminal activity may be afoot and that the persons with whom he is dealing may be armed and presently dangerous, where in the course of investigating this behavior he identifies himself as a policeman and makes reasonable inquiries, and where nothing in the initial stages of the encounter serves to dispel his reasonable fear for his own or others' safety, he is entitled for the protection of himself and others in the area to conduct a carefully limited search of the outer clothing of such persons in an attempt to discover weapons which might be used to assault him. [392 U.S. 1, 31] Such a search is a reasonable search under the Fourth Amendment, and any weapons seized may properly be introduced in evidence against the person from whom they were taken.

Affirmed.

MR. JUSTICE BLACK concurs in the judgment and the opinion except where the opinion quotes from and relies upon this Court's opinion in Katz v. United States and the concurring opinion in Warden v. Hayden.

MR. JUSTICE HARLAN, concurring.

While I unreservedly agree with the Court's ultimate holding in this case, I am constrained to fill in a few gaps, as I see them, in its opinion. I do this because what is said by this Court today will serve as initial guidelines for law enforcement authorities and courts throughout the land as this important new field of law develops.

A police officer's right to make an on-the-street "stop" and an accompanying "frisk" for weapons is of course bounded by the protections afforded by the Fourth and Fourteenth Amendments. The Court holds, and I agree, that while the right does not depend upon possession by the officer of a valid warrant, nor upon the existence of probable cause, such activities must be reasonable under the circumstances as the officer credibly relates them in court. Since the question in this and most cases is whether evidence produced by a frisk is admissible, the problem is to determine what makes a frisk reasonable.

If the State of Ohio were to provide that police officers could, on articulable suspicion less than probable cause, forcibly frisk and disarm persons thought to be carrying concealed weapons, I would have little doubt that action taken pursuant to such authority could be constitutionally reasonable. Concealed weapons create an immediate [392 U.S. 1, 32] and severe danger to the public, and though that danger might not warrant routine general weapons checks, it could well warrant action on less than a "probability." I mention this line of analysis because I think it vital to point out that it cannot be applied in this case. On the record before us Ohio has not clothed its policemen with routine authority to frisk and disarm on suspicion; in the absence of state authority, policemen have no more right to "pat down" the outer clothing of passers-by, or of persons to whom they address casual questions, than does any other citizen. Consequently, the Ohio courts did not rest the constitutionality of this frisk upon any general authority in Officer McFadden to take reasonable steps to protect the citizenry, including himself, from dangerous weapons.

The state courts held, instead, that when an officer is lawfully confronting a possibly hostile person in the line of duty he has a right, springing only from the necessity of the situation and not from any broader right to disarm, to frisk for his own protection. This holding, with which I agree and with which I think the Court agrees, offers the only satisfactory basis I can think of for affirming this conviction. The holding has, however, two logical corollaries that I do not think the Court has fully expressed.

In the first place, if the frisk is justified in order to protect the officer during an encounter with a citizen, the officer must first have constitutional grounds to insist on an encounter, to make a forcible stop. Any person, including a policeman, is at liberty to avoid a person he considers dangerous. If and when a policeman has a right instead to disarm such a person for his own protection, he must first have a right not to avoid him but to be in his presence. That right must be more than the liberty (again, possessed by every citizen) to address questions to other persons, for ordinarily the person [392 U.S. 1, 33] addressed has an equal right to ignore his interrogator and walk away; he certainly need not submit to a frisk for the questioner's protection. I would make it perfectly clear that the right to frisk in this case depends upon the reasonableness of a forcible stop to investigate a suspected crime.

Where such a stop is reasonable, however, the right to frisk must be immediate and automatic if the reason for the stop is, as here, an articulable suspicion of a crime of violence. Just as a full search incident to a lawful arrest requires no additional justification, a limited frisk incident to a lawful stop must often be rapid and routine. There is no reason why an officer, rightfully but forcibly confronting a person suspected of a serious crime, should have to ask one question and take the risk that the answer might be a bullet.

The facts of this case are illustrative of a proper stop and an incident frisk. Officer McFadden had no probable cause to arrest Terry for anything, but he had observed circumstances that would reasonably lead an experienced, prudent policeman to suspect that Terry was about to engage in burglary or robbery. His justifiable suspicion afforded a proper constitutional basis for accosting Terry, restraining his liberty of movement briefly, and addressing questions to him, and Officer McFadden did so. When he did, he had no reason whatever to suppose that Terry might be armed, apart from the fact that he suspected him of planning a violent crime. McFadden asked Terry his name, to which Terry "mumbled something." Whereupon McFadden, without asking Terry to speak louder and without giving him any chance to explain his presence or his actions, forcibly frisked him.

I would affirm this conviction for what I believe to be the same reasons the Court relies on. I would, however, make explicit what I think is implicit in affirmance on [392 U.S. 1, 34] the present facts. Officer McFadden's right to interrupt Terry's freedom of movement and invade his privacy arose only because circumstances warranted forcing an encounter with Terry in an effort to prevent or investigate a crime. Once that forced encounter was justified, however, the officer's right to take suitable measures for his own safety followed automatically.

Upon the foregoing premises, I join the opinion of the Court.

MR. JUSTICE WHITE, concurring.

I join the opinion of the Court, reserving judgment, however, on some of the Court's general remarks about the scope and purpose of the exclusionary rule which the Court has fashioned in the process of enforcing the Fourth Amendment.

Also, although the Court puts the matter aside in the context of this case, I think an additional word is in order concerning the matter of interrogation during an investigative stop. There is nothing in the Constitution which prevents a policeman from addressing questions to anyone on the streets. Absent special circumstances, the person approached may not be detained or frisked but may refuse to cooperate and go on his way. However, given the proper circumstances, such as those in this case, it seems to me the person may be briefly detained against his will while pertinent questions are directed to him. Of course, the person stopped is not obliged to answer, answers may not be compelled, and refusal to answer furnishes no basis for an arrest, although it may alert the officer to the need for continued observation. In my view, it is temporary detention, warranted by the circumstances, which chiefly justifies the protective frisk for weapons. Perhaps the frisk itself, where proper, will have beneficial results whether questions are asked or not. If weapons are found, an arrest will follow. [392 U.S. 1, 35] If none are found, the frisk may nevertheless serve preventive ends because of its unmistakable message that suspicion has been aroused. But if the investigative stop is sustainable at all, constitutional rights are not necessarily violated if pertinent questions are asked and the person is restrained briefly in the process.

MR. JUSTICE DOUGLAS, dissenting.

I agree that petitioner was "seized" within the meaning of the Fourth Amendment. I also agree that frisking petitioner and his companions for guns was a "search." But it is a mystery how that "search" and that "seizure" can be constitutional by Fourth Amendment standards, unless there was "probable cause"[24] to believe that (1) a crime had been committed, or (2) a crime was in the process of being committed, or (3) a crime was about to be committed.

The opinion of the Court disclaims the existence of "probable cause." If loitering were in issue and that [392 U.S. 1, 36] was the offense charged, there would be "probable cause" shown. But the crime here is carrying concealed weapons,[25] and there is no basis for concluding that the officer had "probable cause" for believing that that crime was being committed. Had a warrant been sought, a magistrate would, therefore, have been unauthorized to issue one, for he can act only if there is a showing of "probable cause." We hold today that the police have greater authority to make a "seizure" and conduct a "search" than a judge has to authorize such action. We have said precisely the opposite over and over again.[26] [392 U.S. 1, 37]

In other words, police officers up to today have been permitted to effect arrests or searches without warrants only when the facts within their personal knowledge would satisfy the constitutional standard of probable cause. At the time of their "seizure" without a warrant they must possess facts concerning the person arrested that would have satisfied a magistrate that "probable cause" was indeed present. The term "probable cause" rings a bell of certainty that is not sounded by phrases such as "reasonable suspicion." Moreover, the meaning of "probable cause" is deeply imbedded in our constitutional history. As we stated in Henry v. United States, 361 U.S. 98, 100–102:

> "The requirement of probable cause has roots that are deep in our history. The general warrant, in which the name of the person to be arrested was left blank, and the writs of assistance, against which James Otis inveighed, both perpetuated the oppressive practice of allowing the police to arrest and search on suspicion. Police control took the place of judicial control, since no showing of 'probable cause' before a magistrate was required.
>
> . . . . .
>
> "That philosophy [rebelling against these practices] later was reflected in the Fourth Amendment. And as the early American decisions both before and immediately after its adoption show, common rumor or report, suspicion, or even 'strong reason to suspect' was not adequate to support a warrant [392 U.S. 1, 38] for arrest. And that principle has survived to this day. . . .
>
> . . . It is important, we think, that this requirement [of probable cause] be strictly enforced, for the standard set by the Constitution protects both the officer and the citizen. If the officer acts with probable cause, he is protected even though it turns out that the citizen is innocent. . . . And while a search without a warrant is, within limits, permissible if incident to a lawful arrest, if an arrest without a warrant is to support an incidental search, it must be made with probable cause. . . . This immunity of officers cannot fairly be enlarged without jeopardizing the privacy or security of the citizen."

The infringement on personal liberty of any "seizure" of a person can only be "reasonable" under the Fourth Amendment if we require the police to possess "probable cause" before they seize him. Only that line draws a meaningful distinction between an officer's mere inkling and the presence of facts within the officer's personal knowledge which would convince a reasonable man that the person seized has committed, is committing, or is about to commit a particular crime. "In dealing with probable cause . . . as the very name implies, we deal with probabilities. These are not technical; they are the factual and practical considerations of everyday life on which reasonable and prudent men, not legal technicians, act." Brinegar v. United States, 338 U.S. 160, 175.

To give the police greater power than a magistrate is to take a long step down the totalitarian path. Perhaps such a step is desirable to cope with modern forms of lawlessness. But if it is taken, it should be the deliberate choice of the people through a constitutional amendment. [392 U.S. 1, 39] Until the Fourth Amendment, which is closely allied with the Fifth,[27] is rewritten, the person and the effects of the individual are beyond the reach of all government agencies until there are reasonable grounds to believe (probable cause) that a criminal venture has been launched or is about to be launched.

There have been powerful hydraulic pressures throughout our history that bear heavily on the Court to water down constitutional guarantees and give the police the upper hand. That hydraulic pressure has probably never been greater than it is today.

Yet if the individual is no longer to be sovereign, if the police can pick him up whenever they do not like the cut of his jib, if they can "seize" and "search" him in their discretion, we enter a new regime. The decision to enter it should be made only after a full debate by the people of this country.

Notes

1. Ohio Rev. Code 2923.01 (1953) provides in part that "[n]o person shall carry a pistol, bowie knife, dirk, or other dangerous weapon concealed on or about his person." An exception is made for properly authorized law enforcement officers.
2. Terry and Chilton were arrested, indicated, tried, and convicted together. They were represented by the same attorney, and they made a joint motion to suppress the guns. After the motion was denied, evidence was taken in the case against Chilton. This evidence consisted of the testimony of the arresting officer and of Chilton. It was then stipulated that this testimony would be applied to the case against Terry, and no further evidence was introduced in that case. The trial judge considered the two cases together, rendered the decisions at the same time and sentenced the two men at the same time. They prosecuted their state court appeals together through the same attorney, and they petitioned this Court for certiorari together. Following the grant of the writ upon this joint petition, Chilton died. Thus, only Terry's conviction is here for review.
3. Both the trial court and the Ohio Court of Appeals in this case relied upon such a distinction. State v. Terry, 5 Ohio App. 2d 122, 125–130, 214 N. E. 2d 114, 117–120 (1966). See also, e.g., People v. Rivera, 14 N. Y. 2d 441, 201 N. E. 2d 32, 252 N. Y. S. 2d 458 (1964), cert. denied, 379 U.S. 978 (1965); Aspen, Arrest and Arrest Alternatives: Recent Trends, U. Ill. L. F. 241, 249–254 (1966); Warner, The Uniform Arrest Act, 28 Va. L. Rev. 315 (1942); Note, Stop and Frisk in California, 18 Hastings L. J. 623, 629–632 (1967).
4. People v. Rivera, supra, n. 3, at 447, 201 N. E. 2d, at 36, 252 N. Y. S. 2d, at 464.
5. The theory is well laid out in the Rivera opinion:

"[T]he evidence needed to make the inquiry is not of the same degree of conclusiveness as that required for an arrest. The stopping of the individual to inquire is not an arrest and the ground upon which the police may make the inquiry may be less incriminating than the ground for an arrest for a crime known to have been committed. . . .

. . . . .

"And as the right to stop and inquire is to be justified for a cause less conclusive than that which would sustain an arrest, so the right to frisk may be justified as an incident to inquiry upon grounds of elemental safety and precaution which might not initially sustain a search. Ultimately the validity of the frisk narrows down to whether there is or is not a right by the police to touch the person questioned. The sense of exterior touch here involved is not very far different from the sense of sight or hearing—senses upon which police customarily act." People v. Rivera, 14 N. Y. 2d 441, 445, 447, 201 N. E. 2d 32, 34, 35, 252 N. Y. S. 2d 458, 461, 463 (1964), cert. denied, 379 U.S. 978 (1965).

6. See, e.g., Foote, The Fourth Amendment: Obstacle or Necessity in the Law of Arrest?, 51 J. Crim. L. C. & P. S. 402 (1960).

7. See n. 11, infra.

8. Brief for Respondent 2.

9. See Tiffany, McIntyre, & Rotenberg, Detection of Crime: Stopping and Questioning, Search and Seizure, Encouragement and Entrapment 18–56 (1967). This sort of police conduct may, for example, be designed simply to help an intoxicated person find his way home, with no intention of arresting him unless he becomes obstreperous. Or the police may be seeking to mediate a domestic [392 U.S. 1, 14] quarrel which threatens to erupt into violence. They may accost a woman in an area known for prostitution as part of a harassment campaign designed to drive prostitutes away without the considerable difficulty involved in prosecuting them. Or they may be conducting a dragnet search of all teenagers in a particular section of the city for weapons because they have heard rumors of an impending gang fight.

10. See Tiffany, McIntyre, & Rotenberg, supra, n. 9, at 100–101; Comment, 47 Nw. U. L. Rev. 493, 497–499 (1952).

11. The President's Commission on Law Enforcement and Administration of Justice found that "[i]n many communities, field interrogations are a major source of friction between the police and minority groups." President's Commission on Law Enforcement and Administration of Justice, Task Force Report: The Police 183 (1967). It was reported that the friction caused by "[m]isuse of field interrogations" increases "as more police departments adopt 'aggressive patrol' in which officers are encouraged routinely to stop and question persons on the street who are unknown to them, who are suspicious, or whose purpose for being abroad is not readily evident." Id., at 184. While the frequency with which "frisking" forms a part of field interrogation practice varies tremendously with the locale, the objective of the interrogation, and the particular officer, see Tiffany, McIntyre, & Rotenberg, supra, n. 9, at 47–48, it cannot help but be a severely exacerbating factor in police-community tensions. [392 U.S. 1, 15] This is particularly true in situations where the "stop and frisk" of youths or minority group members is "motivated by the officers' perceived need to maintain the power image of the beat officer, an aim sometimes accomplished by humiliating anyone who attempts to undermine police control of the streets." Ibid.

12. In this case, for example, the Ohio Court of Appeals stated that "we must be careful to distinguish that the 'frisk' authorized herein includes only a 'frisk' for a dangerous weapon. It by no means authorizes a search for contraband, evidentiary

material, or anything else in the absence of reasonable grounds to arrest. Such a search is controlled by the requirements of the Fourth Amendment, and probable cause is essential." State v. Terry, 5 Ohio App. 2d 122, 130, 214 N. E. 2d 114, 120 (1966). See also, e.g., Ellis v. United States, 105 U.S. App. D.C. 86, 88, 264 F. 2d 372, 374 (1959); Comment, 65 Col. L. Rev. 848, 860, and n. 81 (1965).

13. Consider the following apt description:

> "[T]he officer must feel with sensitive fingers every portion of the prisoner's body. A thorough search must be made of the prisoner's arms and armpits, waistline and back, the groin and area about the testicles, and entire surface of the legs down to the feet." Priar & Martin, Searching and Disarming Criminals, 45 J. Crim. L. C. & P. S. 481 (1954).

14. See n. 11, supra, and accompanying text.

   We have noted that the abusive practices which play a major, though by no means exclusive, role in creating this friction are not susceptible of control by means of the exclusionary rule, and cannot properly dictate our decision with respect to the powers of the police in genuine investigative and preventive situations. However, the degree of community resentment aroused by particular practices is clearly relevant to an assessment of the quality of the intrusion upon reasonable expectations of personal security caused by those practices.

15. These dangers are illustrated in part by the course of adjudication in the Court of Appeals of New York. Although its first decision in this area, People v. Rivera, 14 N. Y. 2d 441, 201 N. E. 2d 32, 252 N. Y. S. 2d 458 (1964), cert. denied, 379 U.S. 978 (1965), rested squarely on the notion that a "frisk" was not a "search," see nn. 3–5, supra, it was compelled to recognize in People v. Taggart, [392 U.S. 1, 18] 20 N. Y. 2d 335, 342, 229 N. E. 2d 581, 586, 283 N. Y. S. 2d 1, 8 (1967), that what it had actually authorized in Rivera and subsequent decisions, see, e.g., People v. Pugach, 15 N. Y. 2d 65, 204 N. E. 2d 176, 255 N. Y. S. 2d 833 (1964), cert. denied, 380 U.S. 936 (1965), was a "search" upon less than probable cause. However, in acknowledging that no valid distinction could be maintained on the basis of its cases, the Court of Appeals continued to distinguish between the two in theory. It still defined "search" as it had in Rivera—as an essentially unlimited examination of the person for any and all seizable items—and merely noted that the cases had upheld police intrusions which went far beyond the original limited conception of a "frisk." Thus, principally because it failed to consider limitations upon the scope of searches in individual cases as a potential mode of regulation, the Court of Appeals in three short years arrived at the position that the Constitution must, in the name of necessity, be held to permit unrestrained rummaging about a person and his effects upon mere suspicion. It did apparently limit its holding to "cases involving serious personal injury or grave irreparable property damage," thus excluding those involving "the enforcement of sumptuary laws, such as gambling, and laws of limited public consequence, such as narcotics violations, prostitution, larcenies of the ordinary kind, and the like." People v. Taggart, supra, at 340, 214 N. E. 2d, at 584, 283 N. Y. S. 2d, at 6.

   In our view the sounder course is to recognize that the Fourth Amendment governs all intrusions by agents of the public upon personal security, and to make the scope of the particular intrusion, in light of all the exigencies of the case, a central element in the analysis of reasonableness. Cf. Brinegar v. United States, 338 U.S. 160, 183 (1949) (Mr. Justice Jackson, dissenting). Compare Camara v. Municipal Court, 387 U.S. 523, 537 (1967). This seems preferable to an approach which attributes too much significance to an overly technical definition of "search," and which turns in part upon a judge-made hierarchy of legislative enactments in the criminal sphere. Focusing the inquiry squarely on the dangers and demands of the particular situation also seems more likely to produce rules which are intelligible to the police and the public alike than requiring the officer in the heat of an unfolding encounter on the street to make a judgment as to which laws are "of limited public consequence."

16. We thus decide nothing today concerning the constitutional propriety of an investigative "seizure" upon less than probable cause for purposes of "detention" and/ or interrogation. Obviously, not all personal intercourse between policemen and citizens involves "seizures" of persons. Only when the officer, by means of physical force or show of authority, has in some way restrained the liberty of a citizen may we conclude that a "seizure" has occurred. We cannot tell with any certainty upon this record whether any such "seizure" took place here prior to Officer McFadden's initiation of physical contact for purposes of searching Terry for weapons, and we thus may assume that up to that point no intrusion upon constitutionally protected rights had occurred.

17. See generally Leagre, The Fourth Amendment and the Law of Arrest, 54 J. CRIM. L. C. & P. S. 393, 396–403 (1963).

18. This demand for specificity in the information upon which police action is predicated is the central teaching of this Court's Fourth Amendment jurisprudence. See Beck v. Ohio, 379 U.S. 89, 96–97 (1964); Ker v. California, 374 U.S. 23, 34–37 (1963); Wong Sun v. United States, 371 U.S. 471, 479–484 (1963); Rios v. United States, 364 U.S. 253, 261–262 (1960); Henry v. United States, 361 U.S. 98, 100–102 (1959); Draper v. United States, 358 U.S. 307, 312–314 (1959); Brinegar v. United States, 338 U.S. 160, 175–178 (1949); Johnson v. United States, 333 U.S. 10, 15–17 (1948); United States v. Di Re, 332 U.S. 581, 593–595 (1948); Husty v. United States, 282 U.S. 694, 700–701 (1931); Dumbra v. United States, 268 U.S. 435, 441 (1925); Carroll v. United States, 267 U.S. 132, 159–162 (1925); Stacey v. Emery, 97 U.S. 642, 645 (1878).

19. See, e.g., Katz v. United States, 389 U.S. 347, 354–357 (1967); Berger v. New York, 388 U.S. 41, 54–60 (1967); Johnson v. United States, 333 U.S. 10, 13–15 (1948); cf. Wong Sun v. United States, 371 U.S. 471, 479–480 (1963). See also Aguilar v. Texas, 378 U.S. 108, 110–115 (1964).

20. See also cases cited in n. 18, supra.

21. Fifty-seven law enforcement officers were killed in the line of duty in this country in 1966, bringing the total to 335 for the seven-year period beginning with 1960. Also in 1966, there were 23,851 assaults on police officers, 9,113 of which resulted in injuries to the policemen. Fifty-five of the 57 officers killed in 1966 died from gunshot wounds, 41 of them inflicted by handguns easily secreted about the person. The remaining two murders were perpetrated by knives. See FEDERAL BUREAU OF INVESTIGATION, UNIFORM CRIME REPORTS FOR THE UNITED STATES—1966, at 45–48, 152 and Table 51.

The easy availability of firearms to potential criminals in this country is well known and has provoked much debate. See, e.g., PRESIDENT'S COMMISSION ON LAW ENFORCEMENT AND ADMINISTRATION OF JUSTICE, THE CHALLENGE OF CRIME IN A FREE SOCIETY 239–243 (1967). Whatever the merits of gun-control proposals, this fact is relevant to an assessment of the need for some form of self-protective search power.

22. See generally LaFAVE, ARREST—THE DECISION TO TAKE A SUSPECT INTO CUSTODY 1–13 (1965).

23. See also cases cited in n. 18, supra.

24. The meaning of "probable cause" has been developed in cases where an officer has reasonable grounds to believe that a crime has been or is being committed. See, e.g., The Thompson, 3 Wall. 155; Stacey v. Emery, 97 U.S. 642; Director General v. Kastenbaum, 263 U.S. 25; Carroll v. United States, 267 U.S. 132; United States v. Di Re, 332 U.S. 581; Brinegar v. United States, 338 U.S. 160; Draper v. United States, 358 U.S. 307; Henry v. United States, 361 U.S. 98. In such cases, of course, the officer may make an "arrest" which results in charging the individual with commission of a crime. But while arresting persons who have already committed

crimes is an important task of law enforcement, an equally if not more important function is crime prevention and deterrence of would-be criminals. "[T]here is no war between the Constitution and common sense," Mapp v. Ohio, 367 U.S. 643, 657. Police officers need not wait until they see a person actually commit a crime before they are able to "seize" that person. Respect for our constitutional system and personal liberty demands in return, however, that such a "seizure" be made only upon "probable cause."

25. OHIO REV. CODE 2923.01.

26. This Court has always used the language of "probable cause" in determining the constitutionality of an arrest without a warrant. See, e.g., Carroll v. United States, 267 U.S. 132, 156 , 161–162; Johnson v. United States, 333 U.S. 10, 13–15; McDonald v. United States, 335 U.S. 451, 455–456; Henry v. United States, 361 U.S. 98; Wong Sun v. United States, 371 U.S. 471, 479–484. To give power to the police to seize a person on some grounds different from or less than "probable cause" would be handing them more authority than could be exercised by a magistrate in issuing a warrant to seize a person. As we stated in Wong Sun v. United States, 371 U.S. 471, with respect to requirements for arrests without warrants: "Whether or not the requirements of reliability and particularity of the information on which an officer may act are more stringent where an arrest warrant is absent, they surely cannot be less stringent than where an arrest warrant is obtained." Id., at 479. And we said in Brinegar v. United States, 338 U.S. 160, 176:

> "These long-prevailing standards [for probable cause] seek to safeguard citizens from rash and unreasonable interferences with privacy and from unfounded charges of crime. They also seek to give fair leeway for enforcing the law in the community's protection. Because many situations which confront officers in the course of executing their duties are more or less ambiguous, room must be allowed for some mistakes on their part. But the mistakes must be those of reasonable men, acting on facts leading sensibly to their conclusions of probability. The rule of probable cause is a practical, nontechnical conception affording the best compromise that has been found for accommodating these often opposing interests. Requiring [392 U.S. 1, 37] more would unduly hamper law enforcement. To allow less would be to leave law-abiding citizens at the mercy of the officers' whim or caprice."

And see Johnson v. United States, 333 U.S. 10, 14–15; Wrightson v. United States, 95 U.S. App. D.C. 390, 393–394, 222 F. 2d 556, 559–560 (1955).

27. See Boyd v. United States, 116 U.S. 616, 633:

> "For the 'unreasonable searches and seizures' condemned in the Fourth Amendment are almost always made for the purpose of compelling a man to give evidence against himself, which in criminal cases is condemned in the Fifth Amendment; and compelling a man 'in a criminal case to be a witness against himself,' which is condemned in the Fifth Amendment, throws light on the question as to what is an 'unreasonable search and seizure' within the meaning of the Fourth Amendment." [392 U.S. 1, 40]

(http://caselaw.findlaw.com/us-supreme-court/392/1.html)

3 Understanding *Terry v. Ohio*

The decision of the United States Supreme Court in *Terry v. Ohio* was handed down on June 10, 1968. This case gave us the terminology frequently used to describe a field interview or investigative detention: "Terry stop." That an activity so common and critical in law enforcement is known by the name of the first case in which it was addressed by the Supreme Court gives us an indication of the importance of the case. Almost everything we can or can't do during an investigative stop, its intellectual basis, and its legal analysis comes from *Terry*. As a result, this is the point from which we begin our look at the legal and tactical aspects of field interviews.

Facts of the Case

At about 2:30 in the afternoon of October 31, 1963, Detective Martin McFadden was patrolling downtown Cleveland, Ohio. His attention was drawn to two men, later identified as John Terry and Richard Chilton. McFadden did not know them and could not describe what first drew his attention to them. However, he did testify that he had been a police officer for 39 years, a detective for 35 years of that period, and for 30 years had been working the same area of downtown Cleveland, assigned to look for pickpockets and shoplifters. He testified about his habits of watching people throughout the day and that these two men didn't look "right" to him.

As a result he took a position in a doorway 300 to 400 feet away from the men. The more he watched them, the more purpose he found in continuing to observe them. The two men took turns walking around the same street and returning to the other man, waiting on the corner. Each would walk past some stores, then stop at one and look in the window, go farther down the street, then return, looking again into the same window. They repeated this process five or six times each, about a dozen trips in total. A third man, later identified as Katz, stopped and spoke to them briefly, then walked away on the other street at that intersection. Chilton and Terry continued their previous behaviors, then after 10 to 12 minutes followed the path taken by Katz.

His observations made McFadden suspicious that the men were planning a robbery. He stated that he felt it was his duty to investigate further and that he feared that they might have a gun. McFadden followed Chilton and Terry, and saw them in front of a store talking to Katz. McFadden decided it was time to take action. At this time, he did not have any information about the three men other than his observations. He approached the men, identified himself as a police officer, and asked for their names. The only response was a mumble. McFadden grabbed Terry and spun him around so he was facing the other two. Now with Terry between McFadden and the others, he patted down the outside of Terry's clothing. At this time McFadden felt a gun but was unable to retrieve it. He ordered the men to enter the store, keeping Terry between himself and the others. As they went into the store, McFadden removed Terry's coat and retrieved the gun he had felt in the subject's pocket. He then ordered the men to face the wall with their hands raised, and patted down the clothing of Chilton and Katz. He found a gun in Chilton's coat but did not find any weapons on Katz.

McFadden testified that he only patted down the men to determine if they had weapons and did not put his hands beneath the outer garments of Terry or Chilton until he felt the guns. The record indicated that he never put his hands inside Katz's garments since he did not feel a weapon. McFadden seized the weapons, asked the storeowner to call a police wagon, and the two men were arrested and charged with carrying a concealed weapon.

A motion to suppress was filed in the trial court. The prosecution took the position that there had been a lawful arrest and that the weapons had been seized as a result of the search incident to that arrest. The trial court disagreed, stating that it "would be stretching the facts beyond reasonable comprehension" to conclude that McFadden had probable cause to arrest the men before he patted them down for weapons. Regardless, the trial court denied the motion.

Wisely, the trial court ruled in a manner that predicted the outcome of the Supreme Court's analysis. The judge concluded that Detective McFadden, as a result of his experience, "had reasonable cause to believe . . . that the defendants were conducting themselves suspiciously, and that some interrogation should be made of their action." The trial judge further held that McFadden, purely for his protection, had the right to pat down the outer clothing of the men, as he had reasonable grounds to believe that they might be armed.

Foreshadowing the Supreme Court decision, the trial judge distinguished between an investigative "stop" and an "arrest," between a "frisk" and a full search for evidence. Chilton and Terry were found guilty and appealed. The appeal eventually reached the United States Supreme Court.

The Supreme Court's Concerns

The Fourth Amendment states that "the right of the people to be secure in their persons, houses, papers, and effects, against unreasonable searches and seizures, shall not be violated." Relying on established precedent, the Court stated that this applies as much to a person in public as it does to that person at home. A person is entitled to be free from *unreasonable* governmental intrusion. (The great tension between some portions of the community and the police has its roots in the inexcusably poor communication of the legitimacy of the interference with that freedom and the nature of the circumstances under which an officer can interfere. This, compounded by centuries of other wrongs for which today's police are not responsible, generates a level of resentment that impacts the community's perception of all law enforcement actions. While the questionable or even knowingly false assertions of some groups have made the situation worse, law enforcement is responsible for the vast majority of the communication failures, especially when one considers the greater tensions of the last few years.) Clearly, this applied to Terry as he was walking along the street in Cleveland. As the Court saw it, the question was whether under the facts presented, Terry's right to freedom of movement was violated by an unreasonable seizure.

The Court noted that this presented a difficult problem for them to address. Strong practical and constitutional arguments were being made from two opposing viewpoints regarding the law enforcement activity known as "stop and frisk." One viewpoint drew a distinction between a "stop" and an "arrest." This viewpoint asserted that law enforcement must have the flexibility to briefly detain "suspicious persons," and in the course of doing so, have the ability to pat them down for weapons that might be used against the officers. If this enforcement activity led to evidence that gave probable cause to arrest, then the police should be able to make that arrest, and then conduct a full search incident to the arrest.

On the other side of the argument, it was asserted that police powers must be strictly limited, consistent with the development of the law of search and seizure to that point. It was argued strongly that there cannot be a type of police conduct which does not depend on citizen cooperation, but which at the same time does not amount to an arrest based upon probable cause. The historical purpose of the Fourth Amendment was to require specific justification for any intrusion into protected personal interests, along with a strong system of judicial controls to force compliance with constitutional mandates. Allowing this practice to continue with judicial approval would be unsound. As it is today, tension between law enforcement and those living in the inner city was an important social issue, and the Court noted that as a matter of concern.

The Court's power over any questioned practice is the decision whether or not to allow admission of evidence resulting from it. A ruling allowing the use of the evidence thus legitimizes the practice in question. Applying the exclusionary rule to reject the particular practice serves two important interests. If the practice is unconstitutional, but the evidence is allowed to be used, then constitutional protections become meaningless. In addition, the integrity of the court system is destroyed if lawless governmental conduct is allowed.

However, the Court noted, the exclusionary rule should not be used to exclude the use of lawfully obtained evidence merely because some similar conduct violates constitutional protections. In addition, the rule is not effective if the law enforcement goal of a practice is not criminal prosecution. The rule only comes into play in a criminal court setting. To the extent that harassment of citizens may be occurring, it would not be stopped by the application of the exclusionary rule. A harsh application of the rule in an effort to combat practices that it cannot change is of no value and may frustrate legitimate efforts to fight crime.

The Court went on to note that the broad variety of police–citizen interactions cannot be addressed in one case, and the decision was based solely on the facts placed before the Court. Nothing in its opinion should be construed to be approval of police conduct outside of legitimate investigative behaviors. The court system still retains its obligation to protect citizens from harassing or otherwise improper behavior, or that which is conducted without the objective basis as required by the Constitution. Unlawful conduct and its products must not be tolerated by the judiciary and must be excluded from criminal trials. The Court also said that approval of legitimate investigative techniques based on "ample factual justification" did not prevent the application of other remedies where exclusion will not be appropriate.

The Legal Question

Having defined the rough outline of the constitutional issues involved in investigative conduct, and the social context of the time, the Court framed the specific question of the case as "whether it was always unreasonable for a policeman to seize a person and subject him to a limited frisk for weapons unless there is probable cause for arrest." It was not necessary for the Court to address limitations on police conduct in the absence of probable cause to arrest in other circumstances.

The first issue to be determined in addressing this question was the point at which the Fourth Amendment became relevant. More specifically, the Court had to determine if and when McFadden "seized" and then "searched" Terry. The Court strongly rejected the suggestion based upon use of the words "stop" and "frisk" that actions such as those of McFadden did not constitute a "seizure" or "search":

> It is quite plain that the Fourth Amendment governs "seizures" of the person which do not eventuate in a trip to the station house and prosecution for crime—"arrests" in traditional terminology. It must be realized that whenever a police officer accosts a person and restrains his freedom to walk away, he has "seized" that person. And it is nothing less than sheer torture of the English language to suggest that a careful exploration of the outer surfaces of a person's clothing all over his or her body in an attempt to find weapons is not a "search."

The Court saw two particular dangers in the artificial distinction based upon choice of descriptive words. First, this removed the initial contact between officer and citizen from examination under constitutional standards. Additionally, applying a rigid analysis concluding that contacts were either arrests requiring probable cause, or not capable of being either conducted or examined, made various flexible means of controlling police conduct unavailable. A search that is reasonable as it starts may become unreasonable in the Fourth Amendment sense due to its intensity and scope. The extent of a search must be "strictly tied to and justified by" the facts which justified it.

Accordingly, the Court concluded, the traditional "stop and frisk" theory improperly took the analysis away from the appropriate examination under the Fourth Amendment. The issue to be addressed is "the reasonableness in all the circumstances of the particular governmental invasion of a citizens' personal security." The Court rejected the idea that the Fourth Amendment is not a limiting factor upon police conduct that is less than a full custodial arrest or search.

Terry Was Seized

Applying this conclusion to the facts of the case, the Court stated that there was no question that Detective McFadden "seized" Terry and then "searched" him by acting as he did. The issue that came from that conclusion was then whether it was reasonable for McFadden to have acted as he did. To assess the reasonableness of this action, it was necessary to determine whether the activity was justified when it started and whether it was reasonably related in intensity to the circumstances that justified it at the beginning.

As this case did not involve police conduct subject to the Warrant Clause of the Fourth Amendment, it was not necessary to determine whether "probable cause" existed which justified the seizure and search. The Court was not backing down from its strong preference for warrants and the protection provided by judicial scrutiny. Here, however, the situation was simply not possible to address through the warrant process. The Court recognized that fact patterns of this nature must be dealt with immediately and are presented by the observations of the police officer. As a result, an officer's conduct must be tested against the Fourth Amendment's general prohibition of unreasonable searches and seizures.

What Is Reasonable?

The general principles of reasonableness under the Fourth Amendment are the same, regardless of the setting. Reasonableness is determined by balancing the competing interests of the claimed need to search against the privacy rights of the individual. The governmental interest claimed to justify the intrusion into constitutionally protected areas is the first component to be considered. To justify "the particular intrusion the police officer must be able to point to specific and articulable facts which, taken together with rational inferences from those facts, reasonably warrant that intrusion." The protections of the

Fourth Amendment require that at some point a judge examines the reasonableness of the action taken under the circumstances known at the time. "And in making that assessment it is imperative that the facts be judged against an objective standard: would the facts available to the officer at the moment of seizure or the search 'warrant a man of reasonable caution in the belief' that the action taken was appropriate?" Any lesser standard would not provide protection against violations of constitutional rights.

The first governmental interest to be considered is that of effective crime prevention and detection. The Court accepted without difficulty that this is a sound reason for an officer to approach a person to investigate possible criminal behavior without probable cause to arrest that person. Having considered McFadden's description of the events he saw, the Court stated that it would have been poor performance for an experienced officer who saw such behaviors to not investigate them.

Of greater importance to the Court was whether there was justification for the search for the weapons during the course of that investigation. After considering the potential risks to officers and others, the Court concluded it would be unreasonable to prevent officers from making such a limited examination. In rejecting some of Terry's arguments about the nature and scope of allowable searches, the Court noted the substantial difference between a search incident to arrest and a protective search for weapons. An arrest is a long-term interference with a person's freedom; the protective search is a brief intrusion. In addition, the Court recognized that an officer may well perceive danger long before enough information to justify an arrest, the initiation of a prosecution. (Note that officers are almost certain to have a very different analytical framework to apply to the perception of danger than private citizens do. This is sound, but must be very well communicated in both the criminal justice process and in the communication with the rest of the community.)

The Court then concluded that the proper balance in a case such as this supports the officer having authority to make a reasonable search for weapons for the protection of the officer. The officer must have reason to believe he or she is dealing with an armed and dangerous person. The officer need not be certain, but must have facts that would justify a reasonably prudent person in believing that he or others were at risk of harm. In determining whether the officer acted reasonably, appropriate weight must be given to the "specific reasonable inferences which he is entitled to draw from the facts in light of his experience."

Application of This Rule to the Facts

The Court now considered McFadden's conduct under the principles announced. They concluded that he had adequately described facts and circumstances to the trial judge that would justify a reasonably prudent man in believing that Terry was armed and presented a threat to McFadden. "We cannot say that his decision at that point to seize Terry and pat his clothing for weapons" was the result of imagination, or done for harassment. "The record evidences the tempered act of a policeman who in the course of an investigation had to make a quick decision as to how to protect himself and others from possible danger, and took limited steps to do so."

In addition to whether or not the search was justified, the scope and manner of the search are just as important in determining the reasonableness of the search. The Fourth Amendment imposes limitations not only on the initiation of searches but also on their scope. Evidence cannot be introduced if it was found as a result of a search that was not reasonably related in scope to the justification for the search itself.

In the case of a protective search as conducted by McFadden, its scope must be limited to that necessary for the protection of the officer. The possibility that evidence will be lost cannot be part of the justification for such a search. "The sole justification of the search in the present situation is the protection of the police officer, and it must therefore be reasonably designed to discover guns, knives, clubs, or other hidden instruments for the assault of the police officer."

Detective McFadden's search, and his description of it, met the standard expressed by the Court. He patted down their outer garments and did not place his hands under the outer surface until he felt weapons. As to Katz, McFadden never did conduct a more detailed search, as he did not perceive a weapon in the initial frisk.

4   Lessons Learned

In our efforts to understand the lessons to be learned from *Terry v. Ohio*, we must consider the nature of the United States Supreme Court's role in the American judicial system. The Supreme Court is in most ways an isolated academic institution. It is not a trial court, potentially familiar with the conditions faced by the parties to the case in their daily lives. Millions of cases of all types go through the courts of the various states each year; only about 80 or so will have full oral argument and decisions in the Supreme Court. Very few cases come to the Court without having been considered by two or more lower courts, and then only if there is an issue that is deemed important by enough members of the Court. Because of this process, the information available to the justices is limited to only that which has been preserved by careful presentation to the lower courts.

Officers must communicate well for a variety of reasons, not all of which relate solely to the criminal court process. Our reports and testimony must portray what we saw and did in such a manner that the facts are clear to supervisors, prosecutors, defense attorneys, judges, and jurors in every case. Often, the "real world" is a special case to some of these participants. Judges, especially appellate judges, are among the most insulated from the less polished parts of life, and they have admitted as much. *Grotemeyer v. Hickman*, 393 F.3d 871, 879–880 (2004). Any particular encounter could result in either a criminal or a civil case or both. What litigation may result may not be obvious at the time of any given event. Therefore, the record made at the lowest levels of the court system, or even before litigation commences, must be clear in order to ensure that the facts will be communicated to appellate courts.

The actual work of making and protecting the record that will go up to an appellate court is of course the job of the prosecutor (in a criminal case) or Department/Officer counsel (in a civil case). However, that attorney cannot do that without your part of the work, the reports made long before the attorney becomes aware of the event in question. Trial attorneys are not mind readers; they are part of a team. If the information is not made available in a clear and comprehensive manner from the start, the attorney will do a good job of presenting information only by chance if at all. A great example of the importance of the record on appeal and how that record showed the difference between the claims of a plaintiff and the evidence is *Scott v. Harris*, 550 U.S. 372, 378–380

(2007). Plaintiff's claims of reasonable driving in a case based on use of force to terminate a pursuit were implausible if one is generous: "Respondent's version of events is so utterly discredited by the record that no reasonable jury could have believed him." In the authors' experience, this is a very common occurrence, and there are also very real problems with the (lack of) efforts to correct such disingenuous assertions by plaintiffs.

Relatively minor cases can live a long time, and we cannot assume that the outcome of the case is only meaningful to suspects and victims. Some cases that are legally minor can result in a lot of media coverage, and as we have seen, the popular media and others are increasingly both uninformed and hostile. The quality of reports and other documentation may be vital to the interests of officers, their agencies, and the system as a whole—not because of the legal issues but because of the social perspective. Disinformation has become a major problem, and if our profession does not change enough to recognize and address this problem in a sound manner, the damage will not stop.

Prominent cases that seem to attract a great amount of media and social attention are not necessarily the cases that make a major difference in the law. The *Terry* case is a very good example of this. The testimony of Detective McFadden about his observations and actions during a relatively short period of time are important factors in the Court's decision, which has now been with us almost 50 years.

The actual criminal case against John Terry was relatively minor. It was not a major media event. However, it became one of the most important cases in Fourth Amendment law, validated an important law enforcement tool, and predicted some aspects of other major cases. For example, the Court's insistence on objective analysis has become a critical component of the standards for "seizures" of persons by law enforcement officers. The most important case on use of force (the use of force by law enforcement is analytically a "seizure") in American history, itself a "Terry Stop," cites *Terry* for its foundation, the "objective reasonableness" assessment, rather than a 20/20 hindsight analysis. *Graham v. Connor*, 480 U.S. 386, 396 (1989).

McFadden's Articulation of His "Reasonableness"

The reasonableness of an action under the Fourth Amendment is tested by balancing the governmental intrusion against the citizen's privacy interests. To justify the intrusion, the officer must be able to provide "specific and articulable facts." That is, we must be able to describe perceptions made of things that happened, circumstances that existed, and all of the conditions that existed and contributed to the actions taken. When examined later by a judge, the decision of the officer must be considered against the objective standard of the reasonably cautious person. Good faith is not sufficient.

In addition, lawyers are not cops. Some are very attuned to the working environment of a peace officer; some are not. The quality of a report can impact the quality of the lawyer's work. One of the authors has a significant amount of trial experience and has litigated many suppression hearings. Some lessons were learned the hard way, both by this author and by the officers with whom he has worked. He will admit that based on his experience, certain officer perceptions may not be well enough described, but he may read them between the lines of a report. This is no sounder than ignorance, and it has been a constant battle to perceive and overcome. Officers, like lawyers, must also avoid "jargon" that they might use in less formal communication.

The Court accepted without question that crime prevention and detection is clearly a legitimate governmental interest. McFadden was engaged in both parts of this function throughout the events he described. First, he saw something that drew his attention. He did not know yet what it was, but it made him curious. He followed up on that curiosity. This is important to consider. Experienced law enforcement officers do not have "hunches" in the sense that many would assert. They have better observational skills and a different set of analytical skills or processes based on professionally developed knowledge.

In these circumstances, Detective McFadden was able to stand and watch for the time it took to truly see what actions these men took and then consider those actions in the light of his decades of experience. He suspected based on the facts and his experience that a robbery might be being planned: crime detection. He was engaged in the other part, when after observing and assessing, he approached Terry and the other men. This evolved into crime prevention. The Court's treatment of McFadden's observations and actions is indicative of the persuasiveness of the record of his testimony:

> He had observed Terry, Chilton, and Katz go through a series of acts, each of them perhaps innocent in itself, but which taken together warranted further investigation. There is nothing unusual in two men standing together on a street corner, perhaps waiting for someone. Nor is there anything suspicious about people in such circumstances strolling up and down the street. Store windows, moreover, are made to be looked in.

The Court is aware that this is not at all suspicious behavior and has clearly innocent explanations—in isolation. However, McFadden's continued observation will reveal a different situation.

The Court tells us that the facts that might mean nothing to others might mean something specific to a police officer:

> But the story is quite different where, as here, two men hover about a street corner for an extended period of time, at the end of which it becomes apparent that they are not waiting for anyone or anything; where these men pace alternately along an identical route, pausing to stare in the same store window roughly 24 times; where each completion of this route is followed immediately by a conference between the two men on the corner; where they are joined in one of these conferences by a man who leaves swiftly; and where the two men follow the third and rejoin him a couple of blocks away.
>
> *Terry v. Ohio*, 392 U.S. 1, 23 (1968)

Remember that the Supreme Court is not a trial court. The vast majority of cases that come to this Court have been distilled and considered by many smart minds in several steps before the case is even considered for hearing. Its members are not closely in touch with the practical realities of enforcing the criminal law closer to "the street." Far to the contrary, in fact—they have a relatively insulated existence centered on intellectual pursuits. It would not be surprising if they did not appreciate what this fact pattern might mean to an experienced officer such as McFadden. Given that context, the strength of the Court's next sentence is important: **"It would have been poor police work indeed for an officer of 30 years' experience in the detection of thievery from stores in this same neighborhood to have failed to investigate this behavior further."**

Let's consider that statement for a moment. Being aware of the community or the specific part in which one works is part of real community policing. Real community policing means trying to know who the people in that area are, who acts in a positive manner, who acts in a negative manner, and what specific problems are presented by those whose misconduct makes life difficult for the rest of the people who live there. It is not about pleasing or appeasing those whose conduct needs to be addressed and impeded, but rather it is about helping those impacted by the former group by making their unlawful acts as difficult as lawfully possible.

Reasonableness Applied to the Weapon Frisk

Having easily accepted that McFadden had demonstrated a sound basis for investigating the behavior of the three men, the Court had to consider the much greater level of intrusion in actually trying to determine if Terry was armed. The Court stated that it seemed "clearly unreasonable" to deny that ability to officers where the officer is justified in believing that the subject of the investigation is armed.

Also, having accepted the appropriateness of such a search in theory, the Court then addressed its limits. The Court distinguished this search from that type of search conducted incident to arrest. Those are based on a totally different circumstance, the initiation of a criminal prosecution. The suspect's freedom of movement is almost totally removed. As a result, the search that comes with an arrest serves a variety of purposes not included in the type of protective search conducted in this case. *Florence v. Bd. of Chosen Freeholders*, 132 S. Ct. 1510 (2012); *Maryland v. King*, 133 S. Ct. 1958, 1970–1971 (2013).

The need for a protective search, based on a perception of danger, can arise long before the officer has probable cause for an arrest. As a result, the Court concluded that the proper balance in such a case requires that officers have

> a narrowly drawn authority to permit a reasonable search for weapons for the protection of the police officer, where he has reason to believe that he is dealing with an armed and dangerous individual, regardless of whether he has probable cause to arrest the individual for a crime.

The officer does not have to be certain: **"the issue is whether a reasonably prudent man in the circumstances would be warranted in the belief that his life or that of others was in danger."**

Conveying Reasonableness in the Weapon Frisk Context

Once again, Detective McFadden's performance in this situation contributed to the Court's favorable decision. The Court's question at this point was whether McFadden's conduct was reasonable, which is a two-pronged analysis, requiring assessment of the search at both its start and as conducted:

> And in determining whether the seizure and search were "unreasonable" our inquiry is a dual one—whether the officer's action was justified at its inception, and whether it was reasonably related in scope to the circumstances which justified the interference in the first place.
>
> *Terry v. Ohio*, 392 U.S. 1, 19–20 (1968)

The information McFadden "detailed before the trial judge" would have justified a reasonably prudent person in thinking that Terry was armed and therefore presented a danger. This point and the context in which it was made should be considered very carefully by today's law enforcement professionals.

At the time of the *Terry* decision, it was not commonplace in most parts of the country for private citizens to be lawfully armed. Although in absolute numbers it is still not common, in most of the country, it is perfectly legal to be armed in public in some manner. Many states have enacted laws that mandate the issuance of permits or licenses that make such carrying of firearms legal, and a growing number of states do not even require such permitting. In some areas, the open carrying of handguns is lawful. Such citizens are often armed for many of the same reasons as off-duty officers are. An armed citizen is not automatically in violation of the law.

There have been numerous cases across the country in which officers have operated on such a flawed assumption, and those officers and their agencies have had extremely unpleasant litigation, suppression, and political consequences. Among those cases are *United States v. Black*, 707 F.3d 531, 540 (4th Cir. 2013)("[W]here a state permits individuals to openly carry firearms, the exercise of this right, without more, cannot justify an investigatory detention."); *Northrup v. City of Toledo Police Department*, 785 F.3d 1128 (6th Cir. 2015)(man walking his dog with family and an openly carried handgun could not be stopped based on a 911 call that he was simply carrying it in the open); *St. John v. McColley*, 653 F. Supp. 2d 1155, 1161 (D.N.M. 2009)(openly carried handgun as allowed by state law was not a basis for contact). In two of these three cases, the contact resulted from citizen "complaints" about the lawful conduct. The discomfort of the hypersensitive or irrationally fearful does not change lawful conduct into unlawful conduct, and officers should be very careful to not make the same error.

Officers must understand the difference between the fact of being armed, which is very unlikely to provide a basis for a *Terry* contact in states where one can be lawfully armed, and being armed when contacted for a "Terry stop" based on other factors. Under *Terry*, "a law enforcement officer, for his own protection and safety, may conduct a patdown to find weapons that he reasonably believes or suspects are then in the possession of the person he has accosted." *Ybarra v. Illinois*, 444 U.S. 85, 93 (1979). Note: you cannot automatically frisk that person you have stopped; you must have some reason to believe that he or she is armed. The United States Supreme Court has not changed its view of the issue since, and there are many state and federal cases to the same effect.

After conducting such a frisk, even if the person is lawfully armed, you may disarm him or her. The authors are aware of both pros and cons to such. Generally, of course, a person who has been disarmed is much less likely to present a threat to the officers and bystanders. Some, maybe most, officers are not firearms enthusiasts, as was sometimes the case in the past. When presented with an unfamiliar firearm, the risk of an unintentional discharge by the officer can increase. Both authors are familiar with such circumstances and have assisted other officers in handling unfamiliar firearms. Officers should apply informed judgment to the decision to take a citizen's firearm. At a minimum, if you determine to disarm a citizen for the period of an encounter, you must know and strictly apply the four rules of firearm safety. (One phrasing of those rules is as follows: All guns are always loaded; Never let the muzzle cover anything you are not willing to destroy; Keep your finger off the trigger until your sights are on the target; Be sure of your target.)

What McFadden saw and described resulted in his suspicion that the three men were preparing to commit a robbery, and nothing he saw after he began watching them caused him to have a different viewpoint. Consistent with his suspicion that they were planning a robbery, McFadden suspected that the men were armed. When he made contact with them, again nothing occurred to change his suspicion. It would be sheer insanity to think anything other than that a person who is armed for the purpose of committing a robbery or other crime is not dangerous.

Having supported McFadden's analysis to this point, the Court seems to be favorably impressed with the manner in which he took action to protect himself: "We cannot say that his decision at that point to seize Terry and pat his clothing for weapons" was the result of imagination or done for harassment. "(T)he record evidences the tempered act of a policeman who in the course of an investigation had to make a quick decision as to how to protect himself and others from possible danger, and took limited steps to do so." Note the Court's reference to the record, which is the only source of an appellate court's information about the case. Note also the Court acknowledges that there are very short time constraints under which an officer may have to make a decision and take action, and it assesses McFadden's decision as to how to deal with Terry within that context.

Additional Lessons

Beyond the obvious academic legal lessons of the *Terry* case are some performance issues in which Detective McFadden provided a great example to us.

First, don't be afraid to admit that you can't be sure what drew your attention to some person or situation. Your obligations with regard to reports and testimony require such honesty, and no harm should be done to your case. As an experienced officer described the basis for following up on his curiosity— it's the "SDLR" test: "Something doesn't look right." You need not know what it is immediately, or even why your attention was drawn to that "something." Curiosity is a necessary trait for a skillful law enforcement officer.

Second, be willing to take the time to truly observe, and then analyze, what you perceive. When McFadden became curious, he watched the three men until he had sufficient facts to make a decision as to whether or not the men might be engaged in crime-related behavior. Curiosity is necessary, but so is thoughtful analysis. There is rarely a need to rush into a situation; analysis should precede action. Obviously, the circumstances can dictate the tactics, and there may be an event that requires immediate action. One of our purposes here is to help lay the intellectual foundation that allows the best decision making under all conditions.

Third, do your best to communicate what you saw, what it meant in terms of your training and experience, and what you did. Do this in your reports. It may make a critical difference in the ability of a prosecutor to decide on and justify charges; to present and argue the case; and to persuade jurors, judges, and defense attorneys. The reputation you develop for quality reports and testimony will stay with you and be part of how you and your cases are viewed by every other participant in the criminal justice system. The time invested in your report will allow you to do the best possible communication in your testimony. You will be able to better recall the events that occurred some time ago if your report is written well. Often, the more serious the case, the longer the time until trial, if there is one, so the effort you put into that report will be even more important. Had McFadden in any way acted unreasonably, written a poor report or testified poorly, the outcome of this case might have been much less favorable for law enforcement. We owe his legacy the same professionalism.

5　Evolving Legal Fundamentals

In performing law enforcement duties, you encounter citizens under circumstances involving unusual behavior, some of which may indicate criminal activity. These circumstances span a wide variety of situations and conduct. Depending on the situation encountered, your response may range from a mere contact to a full-custody arrest. (Some may require a totally different viewpoint and response in the nature of a community care-taking function or protective custody, which are outside the scope of this text but critical professional knowledge.) We intend to provide guidance for officer conduct in such street encounters to maximize officer safety and crime suppression with minimal exposure to potential adverse outcomes from judicial and departmental actions.

The "field interview" and other investigative stops can be valuable components of a police officer's public safety and crime control efforts. Appropriate field interviews may provide opportunities to:

1. develop knowledge of a patrol area (people, places, and activities);
2. reduce opportunity for criminal conduct (crime suppression);
3. develop information regarding criminal activity, possibly leading to probable cause for arrest; and
4. demonstrate to the public a commitment to investigate suspicious circumstances.

As noted previously, "stop and frisk" as known today was first considered and accepted by the United States Supreme Court in *Terry v. Ohio*, 392 U.S. 1 (1968). There are two components to this practice: the "stop," which must be of reasonable and brief duration, and the "frisk," which allows an officer to protect him or herself by patting down the outer garments of the person stopped for weapons that might be used against the officer. These are not the same as "arrest" and "search." The "stop" and "frisk" are related but less-intrusive Fourth Amendment concepts. For our purposes in this text, the term "weapon" should be construed broadly, based on decades of professional understanding of what may be used as a weapon by a motivated offender. Remember that many objects can be "weapons," whether or not they are designed for use as such, and whether or not legally possessed. As a realistic matter, the only purpose of such a frisk is to detect a weapon that could be used against the officer, but there is a limited exception. In *Minnesota v. Dickerson*, 508 U.S. 366 (1993), the United States Supreme Court held that an item whose contraband nature is "immediately apparent" may be seized if discovered during a lawful patdown. We believe that this should not be relied upon. Although not impossible, in most circumstances detecting some item, the contraband nature of which is "immediately apparent" in the course of a weapon frisk, is unlikely.

The "stop" component is codified in one state statute that we are using as a model; that statute must be construed in a manner consistent with *Terry* and later cases. A specific statute such as this is not required by the Fourth Amendment as authorization for a "Terry stop," but this state's statute is a useful example of how such a statute (or possibly a policy manual provision) might be worded. Note that although such a statute is not required by the Fourth Amendment, your state constitution and/or court decisions may require some such authorization, which may also hold you to a more stringent standard than that described here. Your state constitution may also have a more restrictive approach to search and seizure. Obviously this book cannot address the details of such state law issues, but you must know them for yourself. As with all issues of law, your department's attorney and your local prosecutor should be working together and heavily engaged in ensuring the best possible training and knowledge. The statute states:

Sec. 107–14. Temporary questioning without arrest.

(a) A peace officer, after having identified himself as a peace officer, may stop any person in a public place for a reasonable period of time when the officer reasonably infers from the circumstances that the person is committing, is about to commit or has committed an offense as defined in Section 102–15 of this Code, and may demand the name and address of the person and an explanation of his actions. Such detention and temporary questioning will be conducted in the vicinity of where the person was stopped.

Some number of states have such statutes. *Hiibel v. Sixth Judicial District Court of Nevada*, 542 U.S. 177, 182 (2004). You must be careful not to consider yourself to have more authority than you actually do. The "reasonable period of time" will vary. In some circumstances, the time needed to complete the stop might be as great as 30 minutes, such as when an officer in a relatively rural area encounters persons matching the facts of some violent offense. Simply controlling the scene until enough other officers are present may take a significant amount of time. Certainly, one should not get in a rush to pursue leads in a manner that is contrary to sound safety practices.

In addition, officers need to make sure that the law believed to have been violated actually exists, and has the meaning it is believed to have. In a very rare event, one that is unlikely to be repeated, a North Carolina officer's mistake as to the law was found to be reasonable. *Heien v. North Carolina,* ____ U.S. ____, 135 S. Ct. 530 (2014). In this case, a sergeant made a stop because the vehicle only had one functioning brake light. Based on the wording of the state law, which used the singular ("a stop lamp"), the state Court of Appeals held that the stop was not valid as there was no actual violation of the law. The North Carolina Supreme Court concluded that the Sergeant could have reasonably believed that the law was as he thought, including because another statutory provision addressing the rear lamps of a vehicle required that "all originally equipped rear lamps" work. After other procedural steps, Heien appealed to the U.S. Supreme Court. Under the circumstances, that Court concluded that the mistake of law was reasonable, which is of course the core of Fourth Amendment analysis. However, the Court did tell us that "an officer can gain no Fourth Amendment advantage through a sloppy study of the laws he is duty bound to enforce." 135 S. Ct. 539–540. One must also consider that such a mistake will only be reasonable once; that is, once the incorrect understanding is known to be incorrect, such an error can no longer be reasonable. The authors believe that a circumstance such as in *Heien* will be very rare, and that based on the Court's caution about sloppiness, officers would be well advised to never expect to have such an error come out in their favor.

Stopping a vehicle for investigative purposes related to a traffic offense is fundamentally a "Terry stop." *Arizona v. Johnson,* 555 U.S. 323, 330 (2009); *Rodriguez v. United States,* ____ U.S. ____, 135 S. Ct. 1609, 1614 (collecting and discussing cases)(2015). As to a vehicle stop related to a traffic offense, the period may be very short. Having a trained canine sniff around a vehicle during the period of a traffic stop **without extending that period** is not unreasonable. *Illinois v. Caballes,* 543 U.S. 405 (2005)(emphasis added). A sniff that required waiting longer than the time needed to address the enforcement issue in order to have backup is unreasonable. *Rodriguez v. United States,* ____ U.S. ____, 135 S. Ct. 1609 (2015). (The authors are not at all encouraging officers to shortcut safety by doing any search without sufficient backup because of time constraints. This is clearly unsound, has resulted in officers being killed, and should be presumed to be a basis for discipline.) Obviously, a driving under the influence (DUI) investigation will take longer than addressing a matter such as an equipment violation. One important consideration is that you must be observant as to all of the facts presented and realize that the encounter can start as one type of event and transition to another. Remember also that anyone in the car is seized for the duration of the stop as well as the driver, so they too could become the subject of investigation as facts develop, and they also will have standing to challenge the lawfulness of the stop. *Brendlin v. California,* 551 U.S. 249 (2007).

As the encounter transitions, you must do so too, and you must be able to properly articulate that transition in any subsequent documentation. For example, it is entirely possible that in the course of a vehicle stop an officer could conclude that any particular occupant of the vehicle is armed and dangerous. *Arizona v. Johnson,* 555 U.S. 323, 332 (2009). If there is in fact such reasonable suspicion, the fact that this is not a consensual encounter will allow for an appropriate frisk. Similar to concerns the authors have expressed with other cases, the Supreme Court questions the prosecution's concession that the encounter was consensual. *Id.* It was not, and Johnson could have been directed out of the car by command and frisked likewise. *Id.*, at 333.

Despite the use of the word "demand" in the statute quoted, the citizen generally cannot be compelled to speak to you, except in circumstances where there is an independent requirement that the person identify him or herself (such as operating a motor vehicle, as the person must be able to prove that he or she is properly licensed). If your state has a statute that mandates that the citizen provide his or her name, then it must be provided, and the failure to do so may constitute a crime. *Hiibel v. Sixth Judicial District Court of Nevada*, 524 U.S. 177 (2004).

If there is no such statute, it is unlikely that the citizen can be forced to provide his or her name or other identifying data. However, even in the absence of such a statute, nothing prevents an officer from asking for identification or other information in the hope that the citizen complies. Refusing to provide identification if there is no independent mandate to do so or displaying an antagonistic attitude is not itself a sufficient basis for an arrest. *People v. Weathington*, 411 N.E. 2d 862 (1980); *Florida v. Bostwick*, 501 U.S. 429, 437 (1991). There is no need to advise the citizen of any "right to remain silent" as there would be in a custodial interrogation (the "*Miranda* warning"). *Berkemer v. McCarty*, 468 U.S. 420, 439–440 (1984).

There are distinctions between merely stopping or temporarily detaining a person, restraining that person (i.e., effecting the stop by some application of force, not merely by presence or display of authority), and arresting that person. Although some of these distinctions are narrow, they can lead to problems related to the use of force issues discussed later; many of the problems presented have become political and social issues despite being legally modest. Certainly, the force used must be "objectively reasonable." *Graham v. Connor*, 490 U.S. 386 (1989). What is objectively reasonable will vary by the basis for the encounter, what you have perceived, and your own capabilities. Of course, when one "obstructs" or "resists" that lawful stop, depending on how your state law is written to describe interfering with the duties of a law enforcement officer, the situation has now shifted and arrest is almost certainly justified. Pre-service training should cover this as with all other legal issues, with regular updates and refresher training throughout one's career.

When a person is stopped by an officer and not allowed to proceed on his way, he has been detained. Obviously, when a person is transported to a police building (jail, headquarters, etc.) or other location under circumstances in which he does not have the alternative to go on his way, then the person has almost certainly been arrested. This requires the officer to have probable cause to believe that an offense has been committed and that this person has committed it. LaFave, Search and Seizure: A Treatise on the Fourth Amendment, 5th ed. (West, St. Paul, 2012) § 9.2g.

The field interview must be used with discretion and good judgment. It must not involve the random or aimless stopping and questioning of citizens, but must be based on reasonable inferences from the circumstances encountered by the officer. **You must be able to relate those observations that caused you to suspect that the person with whom you wish to speak is committing, about to commit, or has committed an offense.**

It is interesting to note that the lack of reasonable suspicion was conceded by the state at some level below the Supreme Court in *California v. Hodari D.*, 499 U.S. 621 (1991). The authors are troubled by the state's concession, as the majority seems to have been. Foreshadowing *Illinois v. Wardlow*, 528 U. S. 119 (2000), the court said:

> California conceded below that Officer Pertoso did not have the "reasonable suspicion" required to justify stopping Hodari, see *Terry v. Ohio*, 392 U.S. 1 (1968). That it would be unreasonable to stop, for brief inquiry, young men who scatter in panic upon the mere sighting of the police is not self-evident, and arguably contradicts proverbial common sense. See Proverbs 28:1 ("The wicked flee when no man pursueth"). We do not decide that point here, but rely entirely upon the State's concession.
>
> 499 U.S. at 623, fn 1

To the authors, this is indicative of a lack of nuanced thinking at the trial level, when the state seems to have conceded that the officers did not have reasonable suspicion as a result of their observations of the conduct, including that the group fled. This concession implicitly acknowledges that the officers should not have been pursuing anyone because they had no reason to. It is difficult to consider that a wise position to assert in describing the conduct of law enforcement officers, as it leaves them arguably exposed to negative administrative or legal consequences. This is especially true when it appears that they may well have had a reasonable basis for such a suspicion. (The suppression of the evidence recovered was reversed because Respondent had not been seized at the time he abandoned the evidence.) Why are we so concerned when the prosecution "won"?

Consider this: Continuing farther into the statute cited above, we find a new subsection (b), effective January 1, 2016:

> (b) Upon completion of any stop under subsection (a) involving a frisk or search, and unless impractical, impossible, or under exigent circumstances, the officer shall provide the person with a stop receipt which provides the reason for the stop and contains the officer's name and badge number. This subsection (b) does not apply to searches or inspections for compliance with the Fish and Aquatic Life Code, the Wildlife Code, the Herptiles-Herps Act, or searches or inspections for routine security screenings at facilities or events. For the purposes of this subsection (b), "badge" means an officer's department issued identification

number associated with his or her position as a police officer with that department.

Although the statute is mandatory, as we see by the use of the word "shall," we do not readily see a penalty for violation. However, that could easily happen and be implemented in several ways. None of them are appealing to any thinking person. The authors strongly suspect that this new subsection is a result of citizen perceptions, communicated to their legislators, that in fact law enforcement was not conducting such stops in a reasonable and lawful manner. Whether or not that perception is correct no longer matters; we are stuck with it, until and unless there is a substantial improvement in how law enforcement agencies communicate their lawful authority and actions. We expect to see further statutory changes in the same direction.

Consider how the concession in the *Hodari D.* case and this statute could interact to cause very bad outcomes for officers, agencies, and the profession. An event during the summer of 2015 resulted in massive rioting, employment consequences, and very questionable criminal charges against officers, largely because of an incorrect assertion that the officers did not have a lawful basis for their contact with a citizen who ended up dying accidentally while in custody. The subsequent acquittals of the first officers tried, followed by the dismissal of the criminal charges and the pending Bar complaint made by a law professor not involved in the matter, are only partial vindication. There is ample information from which one could believe that they have been through a terrible level of stress and may still suffer unjustified career damage. The authors know or know of officers who have experienced similar but not as extreme events and whose health has apparently suffered as a result. As of this writing, the officers' civil suit against those officials responsible for the charges has survived motions to dismiss, an unusual event given the substantial immunities provided to such officials.

The authors have concluded that law enforcement agencies generally seem to do an utterly terrible job of communicating what can lawfully be done, why, and how we implement those powers. This is true across all ranks. Patrol officers should do as much as they can, consistent with safety and call volume demands, to explain to citizens the bases for their actions, preferably during the various opportunities that may arise in other circumstances, but if necessary, after such an encounter.

This is part of true community policing—letting the people we serve know what we can and cannot do for their problems and why. Command personnel need to do the same, on a larger scale. Regular communication efforts, using everything from addressing community groups to newspaper columns to social media information and marketing campaigns are no longer an option, or your Public Information Officer (PIO)'s fantasy. We are not doing well in the contest for hearts and minds, and while the disinformation from various sources, unthinkingly repeated by media outlets, is part of the problem, we certainly have not been part of the solution.

Similarly, we have advocated for years that agencies need to do a better job of collecting information and supporting documentation about stops, and we have been very concerned that the lack of good data and reports was going to have negative effects. A related concern has been that if agencies are collecting good data, it is not being assessed and utilized. We see that as resulting from a lack of resources, often driven by a lack of understanding of the importance of having, validating, and using the data. The apparent validation of this concern by events such as the appearance of this new subsection is not at all gratifying. We have seen truly unsound case decisions based upon data that is used simplistically to assert systemic misconduct. See, for example, *State v. E.J.J.*, 183 Wn. 2d 497 (2015)(Madsen, J., concurring); *Commonwealth v. Warren*, 475 Mass. 530 (2016). A disparate outcome, without considering a much broader set of factors than simply racial characteristics, may well provide a very different answer. See, for example, "In Context—understanding police killings of unarmed civilians," N. Selby, B. Singleton, E. Flosi (2016). Although the authors note that the data available and used for that book is imperfect, it is certainly considered and analyzed as well as possible. The book does demonstrate that while of course the police are not perfect, it more importantly shows that the flaws to which we refer with regard to the collection and use of data do exist and are substantial. Law enforcement must do a far better job of collecting and using data if it is to not only maintain credibility but also truly communicate with the community what is really happening.

The analysis of the justification to stop a person must take into account the totality of the circumstances. You must have facts from which you drew reasonable inferences, and these should lead to a reasonable suspicion that the person stopped is involved in criminal activity. These inferences are not certainties but reasonable conclusions based upon the facts. The ability to develop these inferences from observations comes from training and experience as a law enforcement officer, but may also include other knowledge you have developed through other parts of your life outside of law enforcement. As the Supreme Court has said, "the determination of reasonable suspicion must be based on common sense judgments and inferences about human behavior." *Illinois v. Wardlow*, 528 U. S. 119, 125 (2000)(citation omitted). When the facts and the inferences they support lead to the reasonable conclusion that the person is involved in criminal activity, the officer may make an appropriate investigative stop of that person. A particularly good description of how peace officers develop reasonable suspicion can be found in *United States v. Cortez*, 449 U.S. 411, 412–416 (1981). (Over a period of months, Border Patrol personnel working in an isolated area saw a consistent pattern of shoeprints following a specific path. The same design from one set of shoes was observed each time the tracks were seen. The path ended near a specific milepost on a rural highway, leading to the conclusion that the people involved were picked up by a vehicle. The officers drew a conclusion as to a likely time period for the next group to travel that path and took a position that allowed them to monitor the highway for vehicles that might be suitable for transporting such a group. They did in fact observe and stop such a vehicle, resulting in arrests.) One of the important bases for the ability of the officers to understand the meaning of their perceptions in that case was an understanding of their working environment, an issue to be addressed in more detail later in this text.

The Supreme Court has addressed the difference between the citizen's choice not to cooperate and active evasion: "[U]nprovoked flight is not simply a mere refusal to cooperate. Flight, by its very nature, is not 'going about one's business'; in fact, it is just the opposite." *Illinois v. Wardlow*, 528 U. S. 119, 125 (2000). It should be stated explicitly that it was not solely the fact that Wardlow fled that came into play. The dissenting members of the Court correctly noted that the majority opinion did not hold that flight from an officer was per se sufficient grounds to justify a detention. On this issue, the Court was functionally unanimous.

Wardlow was in a high-crime area when he was seen and then fled. Mere presence in such an area, without more, is of course not a sufficient basis for a stop. However, officers need not ignore the nature of the area in which they make observations. *Wardlow*, at 124 (citation omitted.)

Consensual Contacts (Non-Seizure)

Face-to-face interactions between an officer and a citizen under circumstances where the citizen is free to leave if desired are often referred to as some kind of "consensual" contact. Such a contact might reflect a desire to get to know the people of your patrol area, but it may also be undertaken by an officer who has reason to believe that under the circumstances some investigation of an unusual (not necessarily suspicious) situation is appropriate. The Constitution does not prohibit you from being curious about things you see while on duty. The "feel" of such an encounter should probably be conversational. Unless you have an objective basis to believe that an arrest should be made, or that a more aggressive investigative stop should be made, communication with most individuals should generally begin in this manner. Don't forget that this person may be a witness whose goodwill, cooperation, and information are of great value. You may initiate a contact with a person in any place where you may lawfully be.

Generally, you should make your law enforcement status known as part of initiating contact if you are not in a uniformed assignment. (Obviously, if that citizen is not aware you are a law enforcement officer, he or she may perceive the act of initiating contact with them as rude, or a danger cue, depending on their knowledge and experiences.) Persons contacted may not be stopped or detained against their will, or frisked, and need not answer or cooperate in any way. Officers cannot use any force or coercion in initiating contact or seeking cooperation. Persons who do not cooperate must be allowed to go on their way, although in some circumstances further observation or other action may be appropriate.

(L)aw enforcement officers do not violate the Fourth Amendment by merely approaching an individual on the street or in another public place, by asking him if he is willing to answer some questions, by putting questions to him if he is willing to listen, or by offering in evidence in a criminal prosecution his voluntary answers to such questions. Nor would the fact that the officer identifies himself as a police officer, without more, convert the encounter into a seizure requiring some objective level of justification. The person approached, however, need not answer any question put to him; indeed, he may decline to listen to the questions at all and may go on his way. He may not be detained even momentarily without reasonable, objective grounds for doing so; and his refusal to listen or answer does not, without more, furnish those grounds.

Florida v. Royer, 460 U.S. 491, 497–498 (1983) (citations omitted)

We sometimes use the term "social contact" to describe this type of interaction—one that is based upon some factor(s) that do not rise to the level of reasonable suspicion. The term is used in some parts of the country, and to the extent that it is not known everywhere, it is a reasonably simple term to use as to such encounters. Although it is not a completely precise term, because some such encounters are not truly "social," it is as good as any other label of which we are aware.

In our consideration of this sort of contact with others, we have developed some concerns about how officers engage in and describe them. One is that there have been events in which officers did or should have had suspicions, but they did not perceive or articulate them, and thus did not treat the encounter as actually being a "Terry" encounter. In the alternative, the encounter did start out as a consensual citizen contact, but as the facts developed, it should have been perceived as evolving into a different type of encounter. When the officer's report does not reflect that transition well enough, and the prosecutor does not perceive the nuances (of which there may be plenty) on his or her own, the argument is not likely to be properly focused in such a manner as to educate the judge as to what the ruling should be. (Criminal law and practice are not significant parts of most legal educations, and this usually must be overcome by the individual attorney, in part by learning as much as possible about the "filters" through which the police view their working world.) Related to these views, one should consider that if an encounter results in a criminal proceeding, at some point it became something other than a consensual contact. Knowing and communicating that evolution may be a critical skill.

State v. Harrington, 167 Wn. 2d 656 (2009), is an example of such an event. Some of the legal analysis is specific to Article 1, §7 of Washington's state constitution, which is more restrictive of government authority than the Fourth Amendment. There are still opportunities for seeing how different practices could result in a different outcome in the future.

The phrase's plain meaning seems somewhat misplaced. "Social contact" suggests idle conversation about, presumably, the weather or last night's ball game—trivial niceties that have no likelihood of triggering an officer's suspicion of criminality. The term "social contact" does not suggest an investigative component. However its application in the field—and in this court—appears different.

Harrington, at 664

This is also consistent with the authors' concerns. Many officers in relatively busy areas do not have time to have truly social encounters with citizens. Often, and without making a value judgment about this preference, officers do not care to have such encounters with random citizens. As to this encounter, the Court found that it was a social encounter (legally) as it started. The changing circumstances as the encounter proceeded converted it to a seizure. The final step was the frisk conducted, which the Court held was without the necessary level of suspicion. It converted the encounter into a seizure, one made without a demonstrably sufficient basis. The evidence was suppressed.

The *Harrington* case was not chosen to unfairly critique the officer or the prosecutors involved. It was chosen to show how the nuances of an encounter can escape conscious recognition, even though they are easily perceived in retrospect. First, the officer saw a person out at a relatively late hour (2300), in an area of his city that may be more troubled than other areas. The officer properly considered this to be worthy of more attention and realized he did not have a sufficient basis for a seizure. (Is it possible that the officer would have been better off to merely watch and take in additional perceptions, as Detective McFadden did? We will never know, but it might well be an option to consider.) In the course of conversation, however, the officer learned more and assessed it against his experience. In terms of acting on his perceptions and analysis, and maintaining his own safety, he appears to have been on solid ground. Unfortunately, it appears his subsequent report did not show the transition to what was becoming a reasonable suspicion-driven course of conduct. The prosecutors (whom one of the authors has met and considers to be intelligent, competent attorneys) did not have the benefit of that explanation, and because the nuances of such an event require a more focused type of knowledge than most attorneys and judges have, they appear to have made an imperfect argument. The ruling in that case was troubling but forced by the events as presented. Clearly, in a consensual contact, the officer cannot simply frisk someone because of feeling uncomfortable or unsafe. Such an outcome has also occurred under a Fourth Amendment analysis. *State v. Serna*, 235 Ariz. 270, 331 P. 3d 405 (2014). The contrary outcome in *United States v. Orman*, 486 F. 3d 1170 (2007), would probably not be repeated as it is based at least in part on inquiry about being armed that is not consistent with recent case law. All who may have some role in the system need to learn from the case, and that is the reason it is presented here.

A "stop" is a temporary detention of a person for investigation. This is a "seizure," and therefore subject to the requirements of the Fourth Amendment. A stop occurs when an officer uses his or her authority to compel a person to halt, remain in a particular place, or move a short distance to a nearby location, such as to use a radio or telephone, or for identification purposes. Even a short movement will be held by a court to be reasonable only under limited circumstances, generally for identification, and only where the officer is in fact aware that a crime has actually occurred. W. LaFave, *Search and Seizure: A Treatise on the Fourth Amendment*, 5th ed. (West, St. Paul, 2012) § 9.2g. If a person is under the reasonable impression that he or she is not free to leave the officer's presence, a stop ("seizure") has occurred. Yelling at people to stop, holding an item of their property, blocking their path, and circling them with officers and ordering them out of a car are examples of police actions that courts have found to make the interaction with the citizens a "seizure" (but not necessarily an "arrest"). At one time, pursuing a person would have been considered sufficient to constitute a seizure, but that is no longer the case. W. LaFave, *Search and Seizure: A Treatise on the Fourth Amendment*, 5th ed. (West, St. Paul, 2012) § 9.4d. Note that none of these actions involve the application of force. One is "seized" only when the person submits to the officer's demand to halt or is physically restrained. *California v. Hodari D.*, 499 U.S. 621 (1991). Apparently, then, the above behaviors will result in a "seizure" only if the individual submits or is (intentionally) restrained.

> It is clear, in other words, that a Fourth Amendment seizure does not occur whenever there is a governmentally caused termination of an individual's freedom of movement (the innocent passerby), nor even whenever there is a governmentally caused and governmentally *desired* termination of an individual's freedom of movement (the fleeing felon), but only when there is a governmental termination of freedom of movement *through means intentionally applied.*
>
> *Brower v. County of Inyo*, 489 U.S. 593, 596–597
> (1989)(emphasis in original)

If you reasonably infer from the circumstances that a person is committing, about to commit, or has committed an offense, you may stop that person, whether on foot or in a vehicle, in any public place. This is the legal basis for any such stop; you must have this basis if you take any step to detain a person against his or her will. Reasonable inferences are those based on the specific facts known to you, including information provided by a credible source, considered in the light of your training and experience. You do not have "police intuition," although some use that term. What you have are superior observational and analytical skills related to your police duties, developed by training and experience.

A recent case presents some very interesting facts and practice questions. *Utah v. Strieff*, ___ U.S. ___, 136 S. Ct. 2056 (2016). An anonymous person had reported to a drug tip hotline in South Salt Lake City, Utah, that "narcotics activity" was going on at a particular residence. A detective conducted intermittent surveillance of the residence for about a week, presumably between his other duties. Detective Fackrell observed some number of visitors who arrived and then left within a few minutes. There were enough such visits to make the detective suspect that the tip was sound and the occupants were dealing drugs. *Id.*, slip op. at 6.

One of the visitors was Mr. Strieff. As he left the house and went to a nearby convenience store, Fackrell followed and then detained him. The detective identified himself and asked Strieff what he was doing at the house. As part of the stop, Fackrell of course requested Strieff's identification, then ran the resulting information via dispatch. Strieff had an arrest warrant, and in search incident to the arrest was found to be in possession of methamphetamine. Although the full details of the matter and the ruling would be too much detail for this text, the state conceded at the suppression hearing that the stop was unlawful due to a lack of reasonable suspicion. *Id.*, slip op. at 7.

The authors are not comfortable with the concession. The claimed lack of reasonable suspicion for the stop was that Fackrell had not noticed the time at which Strieff had entered the house and as a result could not show he was a short-term visitor, and that meant that the contact and conversation should have been consensual. *Id.*, slip op. at 15. The authors have discussed this, and also consulted with a friend who is a patrol sergeant, a very experienced gang and drug investigator, FTO, and author. Our collective experience resulted in the conclusion that the odds of anyone not engaged in criminal conduct entering such a location are very small, and that almost certainly there was in fact a sufficient basis for the stop. (Although the Court's ruling on attenuation is beyond our scope, we are also concerned about its soundness in this setting in which the only basis for the knowledge about the warrant was the result of the stop. We have also seen similar concerns expressed by a legal scholar and suspect that he is correct.)

We do know that an anonymous tip merely describing a subject's physical appearance, clothing, and otherwise innocuous or lawful behavior does not provide a basis for enforcement action. *Florida v. J.L.*, 529 U.S. 266 (2000). The facts of that case are now more than 20 years old. The increase in the number of lawfully armed private citizens in the intervening years almost certainly means that the fact that a person is armed, without a lot more, would not justify a law enforcement response. The otherwise innocuous details about the individual were likewise meaningless.

Although information from another person can be sufficient to provide reasonable suspicion, an anonymous tip will seldom be sufficiently reliable to justify a "Terry stop." *Navarette v. California*, ___ U.S. ___, 134 S. Ct. 1683, 1687–1688 (2014) (discussing cases). However, in *Navarette*, the Supreme Court accepted an "anonymous" complaint as being sufficient due to the detailed description of the events and vehicle. After being run off the road, a person called 911 and reported the event and described the pickup, its license plate, and direction of travel. A California Highway Patrol officer stopped the vehicle, which was travelling in the direction stated and at a location consistent with the information. Another officer arrived, and when the two approached the pickup, they smelled marijuana. A search revealed 30 pounds of it. The state prevailed in a suppression hearing at the trial level and was affirmed on appeal. The California Supreme Court declined to hear further appeal, and the U.S. Supreme Court affirmed the lower courts.

The majority relied on the fact that the caller was not in fact truly anonymous due to the taping of 911 calls, and the mandate of federal law and regulations that regardless of caller preference, 911 systems cannot be blocked from receiving caller information. Although not a guarantee of reliability, this would factor into the consideration of whether an officer is justified in relying on information provided in a 911 call. The Court concluded that most potential callers would know that they would not be anonymous, thus discouraging false tips. *Navarette*, ___ U.S. ___, 134 S. Ct. at 1689–1690 (2014). A further detail that is mentioned only in passing is that the caller was in fact not anonymous; she had identified herself by name in the call, which could have been easily matched to the phone number from which the call came. However, neither she nor the dispatcher were present at the suppression hearing for reasons not provided in the case, so the tape was not introduced. All involved proceeded as if the caller was actually anonymous when this was a fiction driven by the resulting inability to introduce the recording. *Navarette*, ___ U.S. ___, 134 S. Ct. at 1687, fn 1 (2014).

There are a few additional points about the potential lessons from *Navarette* that should be considered with regard to training those who collect information on our behalf, and that might be worth incorporating into dispatch software to assist in getting the right information. The protocol for taking information when receiving a call for assistance, whether through a 911 system or a non-emergency number, should have a reasonably detailed script that ensures collecting the necessary details for the officers who have to act on that information. In addition, the information obtained as a result of the technology driven by the federal mandates should be included in the information entered into the dispatch record of the incident. Patrol personnel and trainers familiar with the nature of the information needed should be primary resources for the design of this protocol, and case law should be reviewed to ensure that the team knows what information must be sought to make it as likely as possible that action taken in reliance on the information is sound. Subject matter experts in verbal communication should be consulted to make sure that the questions are not confusing and will result in the necessary information. Joint development and training must involve patrol personnel and dispatch/communication personnel.

Officer Conduct During a Stop

Every time you make a stop, you must be prepared to cite those factors that lead you to believe that the stop was justified. The report you'll be writing later must communicate your decision making process to others who weren't there, didn't see what you saw, probably don't have your professional knowledge, and may be critical of your actions, including command officers, prosecutors, defense attorneys, judges, and jurors. **Quality report writing is critical.** The same considerations will also apply to any frisk that you may determine to be appropriate after making the stop.

Proper justification for a stop does not permit unreasonable conduct during the stop—reasonableness is the essence of Fourth Amendment analysis. Every phase of a stop may be reviewed by the courts, command, and others, at a later time if the stop or any part of the encounter is alleged to have been conducted in an unreasonable manner. Unreasonable stops are unlawful, and any resulting evidence will be suppressed. In some cases, unreasonable conduct could result in disciplinary action or civil or criminal liability.

A person stopped may be detained at or near the scene of the stop for a reasonable period of time. Officers should detain a person only for that period of time necessary to obtain or verify the person's identification, account of the situation, or otherwise determine if the person should be arrested, released, or processed in another manner. **There is no per se length of detention rule in these circumstances.**

> In assessing whether a detention is too long in duration to be justified as an investigative stop, we consider it appropriate to examine whether the police diligently pursued a means of investigation that was likely to confirm or dispel their suspicions quickly, during which time it was necessary to detain the defendant.
>
> *United States v. Sharpe*, 470 U.S. 675, 686 (1985)

Your courts may have considered this issue, and the opinions of your state courts may provide guidance; consult your local prosecutor or department legal advisor before this becomes an issue. Note that the Supreme Court tried to allow for the fact that you may encounter widely varying circumstances, so they did not give a specific time limit. Your ability to check the circumstances may vary for reasons beyond your control, but you should probably be very hesitant about detaining someone against his or her will for more than a few minutes without a good reason.

Citizens have to be treated reasonably during stops and similar encounters; of course, what you and citizens consider reasonable will differ, as we increasingly see. Some citizens will not be receptive to procedures necessary for officer safety. **It is better to err on the side of safety and offend someone than to risk your life. If it is your perception that you will not be supported or will be exposed to negative action for sound conduct, consider not making the stop.**

If you have a proper legal basis for the stop, tactically sound safety procedures should not provide a valid basis for legal or disciplinary action against you, regardless of anyone else's feelings or beliefs, or department policies. It is easy to defend an officer who, having an otherwise proper legal foundation for his or her actions, violates a tactically unsound policy. The law is clear and has been this way for several decades. "The risk of harm to both the police and the occupants is minimized if the officers routinely exercise unquestioned command of the situation." *Michigan v. Summers*, 452 U.S. 692, 702–703 (1981). This is true in any non-consensual encounter. *Brendlin v. California*, 551 U.S. 249, 258 (2007)(citations omitted). The existence of any policy directive inconsistent with these cases, or any attempt to impose discipline for violating such a policy, is inexcusable and should result in severe discipline against any involved in developing, approving, or attempting to enforce that policy.

If you are not in uniform, identify yourself as a police officer and give some plausible explanation of the stop as soon as possible. Each officer, based on the areas in which they work, will find different approaches to the explanation to be useful. You may find it appropriate to inform the person that he or she is not under arrest and will be detained only long enough to determine the circumstances. Certainly, officers should generally explain the stop and the basis for their actions to the citizen as part of ending the encounter. Although it may not solve or head off every possible negative response to the officer and the agency, it can't hurt, and may be part of "selling" the stop as lawful and appropriate.

You can ask questions of the person, in the vicinity of the stop, for the purpose of obtaining identification and an explanation of the situation (their presence, conduct, etc.). Citizens maintain their rights under suspicious circumstances, and they probably cannot be compelled to answer these questions or provide identification, except where there is independent statutory basis for requiring identification (such as operation of a motor vehicle, possession of firearms, etc.).

Although the *Hiibel* decision leads some to a different conclusion, the compelled production of identification is not a settled question. *Hiibel v. Sixth Judicial District Court of Nevada*, 542 U.S. 177 (2004). Generally, mere presence in a public place, even when combined with a reasonable suspicion of criminal activity, is not a sufficient basis to require a citizen to provide identification. This may create severe practical problems. For example, the ability to accurately identify a suspect is a major factor in the ability to solve crimes. If only compelled to give their name, and not prove their true identity, it is readily apparent that persons contacted will often provide false names, an experience common to every police officer, including the authors. A leading scholar in Fourth Amendment research has critiqued the position that there is no constitutionally sound way to compel a suspect to provide accurate identification and has suggested that a frisk for identification, similar to the frisk for weapons, might be allowable. A limited frisk as suggested above would reduce the intrusion into potentially protected privacy interests that would result from arrest and criminal prosecution. W. LaFave, *Search and Seizure: A Treatise on the Fourth Amendment*, 5th ed. (West, St. Paul, 2012) § 9.6g.

The *Hiibel* decision does not support the position that there is a blanket obligation to identify oneself in an investigative detention, especially using a particular form of identification. First, the (U.S.) Supreme Court applied

Nevada law as construed by the Nevada courts. The statute in question mandated that a person stopped in an investigative detention identify him or herself and provided a criminal penalty for failing to do so. The Nevada Supreme Court had interpreted the statute to mean that a person was only required to provide his or her name. *Hiibel v. Sixth Judicial District Court of Nevada*, 542 U.S. 177, 185 (2004). As we all know, that is not generally sufficient information for performing all of the database inquiries necessary for both safety and investigative purposes. Most of the time, we need the first and last names, with at least the middle initial, and a complete date of birth, and obviously, a valid form of identification with a photo is preferred.

Additionally, the (U.S.) Supreme Court relied on that statute as interpreted by the Nevada Supreme Court in coming to its decision; the statute as applied did not violate the Fourth Amendment. The Court noted favorably that the Nevada statute was narrower and more precise than a California statute it had previously found unconstitutionally vague. *Hiibel v. Sixth Judicial District Court of Nevada*, 542 U.S. 177, 184 (2004)(citation omitted). That statute had required "credible and reliable" identification. Without being able to compel a person to provide some form of identification upon which we can rely, the value of this case is limited. Furthermore, it appears from reading the case that it is only of significant value in the states having statutes similar to Nevada's. *Hiibel v. Sixth Judicial District Court of Nevada*, 542 U.S. 177, 187 (2004).

The lack of a statute is possible to overcome, if state legislatures are able to be persuaded to enact something of that nature. However, if one need only identify themselves by name, then the authority recognized in *Hiibel* is of limited value. In a case in which an officer compels a person to provide more useful information, or more likely, arrests the person for failing to do so, the cases as they stand do not favor the ability to compel identification that is useful. Although in the future the Court may be receptive to this practical problem, the language of this opinion makes that harder to expect. Officers may be able to compensate for this by various tactics. One is that of running the license plates of any possibly associated vehicles. In at least some states, the driver's license record of the registered owner(s) will return with the registration; if this is not the situation in your state, your professional associations need to do some aggressive lobbying. In addition, of course, your local computer system may provide further data from a name check, but this will only work with local persons who have been previously contacted and identified, and who do not have common names. Then there are those who simply provide a useful form of identification when asked for their name. Be grateful for their cooperation!

Refusal of the person stopped to answer questions or otherwise cooperate is not a crime and does not by itself establish probable cause for arrest. *United States v. Mendenhall*, 446 U.S. 544 (1980). Flight from an officer and failure to give correct identification are not proof of guilt, but such actions may be considered along with other facts known as contributing to probable cause, if under the circumstances, an innocent person could reasonably be expected to cooperate. However, unprovoked flight from officers may be considered with other factors when determining if there is an adequate basis for a stop. See *Illinois v. Wardlow*, 528 U.S. 119 (2000). Even if you aren't sure that you have probable cause for arrest, the refusal may be cause for further investigation of the circumstances, but the period and other conditions of the stop must still be reasonable, considering the facts known to you.

Section II

Blending Law, Policing, and the Community

6   Force and Control

Force is a term of physics, not law. See, for example, the first definition at www.merriam-webster.com/dictionary/force, which generally refers to "strength or energy exerted or brought to bear: cause of motion or change: active power." The legal concept is not "force" as a stand-alone definition. The *application* of such force is the legal concept referred to as "use of force." The lawful use of force is one of the means by which peace officers impose control over others, as they are allowed to do as a matter of law.

The recent commentary about police use of force in this country has been badly flawed. These issues need to be presented accurately and objectively, not emotionally. Along with others, law enforcement managers have overwhelmingly failed in that duty.

Very few people in this country have any idea what criminals are like. Some percentage of the most violent criminals really are unlike most decent people. As one experienced police officer said about criminal conduct and how their mindset differs from that of most others:

> They don't think like us. You're using your window or perspective on the world and overlaying it on what you think criminal scum should think. This is dangerous. Never imagine that they think like you: that they have compassion, that your life means anything at all, that children shouldn't be raped and old people beaten. There are monsters among us, not from Hollywood nor Steven King's mind, but demons in skin suits. They look like us, make no mistake, but they are not us.
> Sgt. Patrick Aherne, personal conversation, 03/31/2017

A similarly large majority of the community also have no knowledge of the law about use of force and what threat perception and management entail. Attorneys, including criminal practitioners, are within this ignorant majority. Few are qualified to assess law enforcement use of force as it is a very specific, arcane subset of knowledge. Unfortunately, disingenuous plaintiff's attorneys and poor responses from those representing law enforcement have resulted in very troubling case law from the Federal Circuit Courts.

Police officers get to control their professional encounters. This may mean among other options using our presence, threatening the use of force, or imposing physical control against the wishes of the subject. The law is clear, and has been this way for several decades. "The risk of harm to both the police and the occupants is minimized if the officers routinely exercise unquestioned command of the situation." *Michigan v. Summers*, 452 U.S. 692, 702–703 (1981). This is true in any non-consensual encounter. *Brendlin v. California*, 551 U.S. 249, 258 (2007)(citations omitted). The statutes of most, if not all, states have the same effect.

One duty of law enforcement officers is to hunt and capture people who do bad things, document the investigation, and send the documentation to prosecutors for consideration of the next steps in the process. Much crime is ugly, sudden, and violent; often, so is controlling the offenders. Only the criminals, through their non-compliance or outright refusal to comply, are responsible for the use of force, despite the claims of the ignorant and hostile.

> Other than random attacks, all such cases begin with the decision of a police officer to do something, to help, to arrest, to inquire. If the officer had decided to do nothing, then no force would have been used. In this sense, the police officer always causes the trouble. But it is trouble which the police officer is sworn to cause, which society pays him to cause and which, if kept within constitutional limits, society praises the officer for causing.
>
> *Plakas v. Drinski*, 19 F. 3d 1143, 1150 (1994)

Law enforcement is not a people-pleasing business; it is a coercive compliance business. The ugly nature of the lawful use of force is a fact, but "ugly" and "unreasonable" are not at all synonymous. The offender may be hurt because of his or her own actions, but any outrage must be directed at the offender, not the police officer who is fulfilling his or her duty. Of course, on the rare occasions that there is actually excessive force used, the officer would be the responsible party.

Officers must always use more force than the offender, and it is the offender who is mandated by law to "deescalate." There is no basis in law or ethics for a policy more restrictive than that required by the law, or to "deescalate" in the face of resistance. Policy directives of such nature are improper and justify substantial discipline; they turn the priority of life on its head by placing the well-being of offenders above that of officers and uninvolved citizens. Such restrictions damage the "delicate balance the Constitution strikes between the dangerous and the endangered," thus thwarting the purpose of the law and undermining the safety of the community and its law enforcement officers. Urey W. Patrick and John C. Hall, *In Defense of Self and Others—Issues, Facts & Fallacies: The Realities of Law Enforcement's Use of Deadly Force*, p. 411 (3rd edition, 2017).

This is not merely the position of those associated with law enforcement. The Supreme Court takes a similar view: "(W)e are loath to lay down a rule requiring the police to allow fleeing suspects to get away whenever they drive so recklessly that they put other people's lives in danger. It is obvious the perverse incentives such a rule would create." *Scott v. Harris*, 550 U.S. 372, 385 (2007). Unenforced laws become mere suggestions.

The standard is simple, and a matter of constitutional law; analytically the use of force is a form of seizure under the Fourth Amendment. The officer must be "reasonable" under the circumstances. Being factually correct is not the standard, nor would it be sound. Whatever the offender is in any other portion of their life, and before the moments leading up to the use of force, is simply not relevant to the analysis unless a history of violence is known to the officer(s). There are occasional events that have been revealed to be truly unfortunate, the result of facts that were not what they reasonably appeared at the time. Sad, tragic, and many other adjectives apply to such events, and they are understandably traumatic to all involved, including the officers. That does not make the officers' conduct "wrong." All that matters is the officers' perception and conduct at the time force is used, assessed through the insight and experience of the officers involved.

Graham v. Connor, 490 U.S. 386 (1989), itself a case resulting from an investigative detention ("Terry stop"), explains the analysis of the use of force in making an arrest or "Terry stop." The test to be used is the reasonableness test of the Fourth Amendment:

> Where, as here, the excessive force claim arises in the context of an arrest or investigatory stop of a free citizen, it is most properly characterized as one invoking the protections of the Fourth Amendment, which guarantees citizens the right "to be secure in their persons . . . against unreasonable . . . seizures" of the person.
>
> 490 U.S. at 394

> The "reasonableness" of a particular use of force must be judged from the perspective of a reasonable officer on the scene, rather than with the 20/20 vision of hindsight. See *Terry v. Ohio*, supra, at 392 U. S. 20–22. The Fourth Amendment is not violated by an arrest based on probable cause, even though the wrong person is arrested, *Hill v. California*, 401 U. S. 797 (1971) . . .
>
> 490 U.S. at 396

The test is not based on hindsight, the ugliness of any significant use of force, or the ignorance of reporters, friends of the offenders, or others unqualified to assess the matter. The Court continues to reject subjective assessment of seizures. *Brendlin*, 551 U.S. at 260.

> The calculus of reasonableness must embody allowance for the fact that police officers are often forced to make split-second judgments—in circumstances that are tense, uncertain, and rapidly evolving—about the amount of force that is necessary in a particular situation.
>
> 490 U.S. at 396–397

Any given situation is likely to be "tense, uncertain, and rapidly evolving." The specific facts that are observed and can be described objectively, and the logical conclusions or meanings to be gleaned from those facts by a reasonable officer on the scene, can be *very* subtle or nuanced, and we need to accept that there is no one-size-fits-all answer to any scenario. The further difficulty presented by second-guessing is similar to that with the "legal analysis" by unqualified individuals. Very few people have any training about the perception and management of threats to their safety presented by criminal actors; even fewer know the applicable legal standards and how they are linked. We have made a conscious decision to address only the most significant cases of the United States Supreme Court. This is driven in part by the need to keep the discussion straightforward, in part because the lower courts have made numerous decisions that cannot be reconciled with those of the Supreme Court, and in part because the Supreme Court has become more vigorous in recent years in its reminders to the lower courts that their rulings are not consistent with the Court's pronouncements. See, for example, *White v. Pauly*, ___ U.S. ___, 137 S. Ct. 548 (2017), and the cases cited therein.

Use of force in a *Terry* encounter is an area full of nuances and relatively few bright lines. The determination requires a careful balancing of "'the nature and quality of the intrusion on the individual's Fourth Amendment interests'" against the countervailing governmental interests at stake. *Graham v. Connor*, 490 U.S. 386, 396 (1989)(citation omitted). The United States Supreme Court recognizes that you must have the ability to use some force to detain a person; to have the authority to detain someone in a *Terry* encounter without the corresponding ability to use force to accomplish the detention would render the authority virtually useless. W. LaFave, *Search and Seizure: A Treatise on the Fourth Amendment*, 5th ed. (West, St. Paul, 2012) § 9.2d. "Our Fourth Amendment jurisprudence has long recognized that the right to make an arrest or investigatory stop necessarily carries with it the right to use some degree of physical coercion or threat thereof to effect it." *Graham v. Connor*, 490 U.S. 386, 396 (1989)(citation omitted).

Reading *Terry* shows that the detective (McFadden) grabbed Terry, "spun him around so that they were facing the other two, with Terry between McFadden and the others" at the beginning of the encounter, after making his observations. *Terry v. Ohio*, 392 U.S. 1, 7 (1968). Although the Supreme Court accepted the officer's actions, the *Terry* decision should not be considered blanket authorization to lay hands upon persons encountered under suspicious circumstances. Detective McFadden's testimony, and presumably his report, painted a picture that not only showed the suspicious nature of the actions of Terry and his associates but also gave the basis for his belief that they could be armed. The "grabbing" may have been allowed, not for the purpose of making the stop, but because McFadden had to take steps to make the protective frisk for a weapon. Based on the lessons of the last 50 or more years, it is probable that a higher level of control (additional officers, drawn and probably pointed firearms, etc.) should have been imposed. Whatever the analytical basis underlying the Court's approval in *Terry*, you must convey the circumstances and the perceptions that result from your professional knowledge to justify the basis for the actions. What you learn later will not be part of the assessment; it is based solely on what you could observe and describe at the time of the event.

A stop of this type is not an arrest, so the provisions of state statutes covering use of force in *making an arrest* do not apply, although they may give some guidance. See, for example, 720 ILCS § 5/7–5. There is no statute in Illinois that applies to the use of force in a "stop and frisk" situation. Another state's (Washington) statutes, however, appear to make such allowance for use of force in a "Terry stop":

> The use, attempt, or offer to use force upon or toward the person of another is not unlawful in the following cases: (1) Whenever necessarily used by a public officer in the performance of a legal duty, or a person assisting the officer and acting under the officer's direction.
>
> RCW 9A.16.020

This is broadly enough worded that it appears to cover both arrests and lesser forms of seizure, but no cases addressing this specific issue appear to have been decided. One must know what the law is in the state in which one works; while the Constitutional standard will generally be reflected in state statutes and case law, there may be deviations in your state law.

The authors discovered a new statute in Illinois while conducting research for the most recent updates to this text:

(720 ILCS 5/7–5.5)
Sec. 7–5.5. Prohibited use of force by a peace officer.

(a) A peace officer shall not use a chokehold in the performance of his or her duties, unless deadly force is justified under Article 7 of this Code.
(b) A peace officer shall not use a chokehold, or any lesser contact with the throat or neck area of another in order to prevent the destruction of evidence by ingestion.
(c) As used in this Section, "chokehold" means applying any direct pressure to the throat, windpipe, or airway of another with the intent to reduce or prevent the intake of air. "Chokehold" does not include any holding involving contact with the neck that is not intended to reduce the intake of air.

We noticed several interesting aspects to this statute. The first is the obvious connection to a very high-profile incident in the summer of 2014 in which a suspect died while resisting arrest. There were many references to the death in which causation was attributed to a "chokehold." In reviewing video of the incident, the authors independently concluded that the contact with the area of the suspect's neck was not only very brief but not at all a "chokehold." Calling that technique a "chokehold" was at best inaccurate, certainly incorrect, and arguably disingenuous. The technique was also not any type of technique in which the blood supply to the brain is temporarily cut off, often referred to as a Lateral Vascular Neck Restraint, or LVNR. It was in fact a leverage technique being used in an effort to control a resistive subject and get him off his feet so that the obviously smaller and lighter officer could control him. The popular mythology is based upon disinformation, irresponsibly repeated.

We did notice that there appears to be a reasonable effort in the quoted statute to distinguish and only prohibit something that is intended to impede airflow and also has a real risk to the structure of the neck. The definition of "chokehold" in this statute would not address either a leverage technique or the LVNR. The authors do believe that a true "chokehold," especially applied by an officer who has been engaged in a physical conflict and who thus has a lot of adrenaline circulating, could easily do enough harm to be legitimately considered force likely to cause death or great bodily harm.

How do you determine the force to use initially? Blocking their path, grabbing the suspect using a "come-along" or other leverage technique, making other physical contact, or a similar low-level use of force is almost certainly justifiable. Certainly, the decision in *Terry* supports such a conclusion. The nature of the criminal activity suspected and the information known about the person will be critical here. If one is investigating a possible robbery, as McFadden was, or dealing with a person known to have a violent history, then the level of force to be used or threatened is likely to be much higher than that used when initially contacting a pedestrian who crossed against the light. Evasion cannot be considered resisting arrest until you are making an arrest, although your state statutes likely have a provision that applies to such a situation and would criminalize the conduct. Such a provision could include language such as California's: "Every person who willfully resists, delays, or obstructs any public officer, peace officer . . . in the discharge or attempt to discharge any duty of his or her office or employment." Cal. PC §148(a)(1); or Washington's: "A person is guilty of obstructing a law enforcement officer if the person willfully hinders, delays, or obstructs any law enforcement officer in the discharge of his or her official powers or duties." RCW 9A.76.020(1). This requires a physical act. Of course, once they are placed under arrest for the acts of obstruction and failure to comply, they are likely "resisting arrest" under this language: "A person is guilty of resisting arrest if he or she intentionally prevents or attempts to prevent a peace officer from lawfully arresting him or her." RCW 9A.76.020(1).

Obviously, force that is likely to cause higher levels of injury, such as a nightstick impact, canine bites, or the discharge of a firearm, should only be used as reasonably necessary to control the situation. An unreasonable use of force may provide a basis for disciplinary, civil, or criminal action. The best defense to such actions against an officer is complete knowledge of the legal basis of your authority, reasonable efforts to determine the factual situation, and sound tactical training and behavior.

Specific answers to the issues raised here are too difficult to predict in a text such as this, considering the wide variety of conditions that may be encountered. Because a "Terry stop" is a Fourth Amendment "seizure," the use of force issue will be controlled by the "objective reasonableness" standard of

Graham v. Connor, 490 U.S. 386 (1989). Under this standard, an officer's use of force to make an arrest or other seizure must be "'objectively reasonable' in light of the facts and circumstances confronting them." 490 U.S. 386, 397 (1989). This is another example of an area in which your department's legal advisor(s), control tactics instructor(s), and other training resources should work together to develop procedures that reflect the law and realistic, validated tactics and techniques. It may not be perfect, but that is not the standard; it must be "reasonable."

If you have a reasonable basis for believing that the person whom you wish to stop is armed or sufficiently non-compliant to present a threat to your safety, you may use such force as is reasonably necessary to make the stop and control the person during the frisk. Your report must clearly show your basis; the need for quality report writing cannot be overemphasized. Display of firearms, use of handcuffs, and use of cars to box in suspects do not necessarily convert a "stop" into an arrest, if the actions were "objectively reasonable" under the circumstances. At some point, an arrest will be found to have been made as a result of the display or application of high levels of force, especially if these higher levels are not justified by the facts communicated to the court, usually in a suppression hearing. W. LaFave, *Search and Seizure: A Treatise on the Fourth Amendment*, 4th ed. (West, St. Paul, 2012) § 9.2d. The court decisions on such issues are driven by minor factual distinctions and to some extent by the quality or lack thereof in the reports of officers and the associated legal arguments. Because of the higher level of intrusion, you must be able to justify such actions; officer safety is obviously the most likely justification. The justification is not a result of the use of the two words "officer safety" or similar simplistic language, but by demonstrating in your reports and testimony how the circumstances and your perceptions raised the level of concern for your safety.

It has been the experience of the authors that officer conduct in use of force and other circumstances is not often a problem. Overwhelmingly, officers are doing their jobs well when it comes to performing tasks. Unfortunately, the same is not always true with regard to report writing, and we do sometimes see cases in which an argument can be made that the officer(s) did something wrong because their report does not adequately describe their actions. This is an important issue, but the testing, hiring, training, and supervision issues related to it are outside of the scope of this text.

In a situation where an isolated officer in a rural area stopped two men matching the descriptions of suspects in a residential burglary that occurred nearby about 30 minutes earlier, approached them with his gun drawn, made them lie on the ground, and handcuffed them after backup arrived while other officers brought an eyewitness to view them, the court stated:

> (t)he permissible bounds of an investigatory stop must be flexible enough to permit a restraining officer to take the least intrusive measures necessary within the dictates of reasonable prudence for his own protection to

maintain the status quo and to diligently pursue a means of investigation that is likely to confirm or dispel his suspicions quickly.

> *People v. Paskins*, 154 Ill. App. 3d 417 (App. 3 Dist. 1987), app. denied 115 Ill. 2d 547 (1987), cert. denied 484 U.S. 868 (1987)

(The officers' conduct was upheld, and the encounter was not at that point considered an arrest despite the higher level of intrusion. As shown by this case, courts will generally be supportive of us when we give them complete information, as a result of which they can make better decisions that are more reflective of an understanding of what we do.) The trial court had correctly determined that such offenders should be presumed to be violent, and thus, the gunpoint contact was tactically appropriate.

If a stop has a legally and factually valid basis, reasonable force used (or displayed) for control of the encounter, including officer protection, will not provide a basis for action against the officer. Force used for any other purposes may be far more difficult to justify. One seemingly common response of the courts to what they consider higher than appropriate levels of force is to consider the event an arrest, rather than a *Terry* encounter. This can be a mixed blessing, depending on the judicial ruling as to whether or not probable cause for arrest existed at the time of the encounter. (A judicial finding that probable cause did not exist for what is concluded was an arrest can have far broader negative consequences than just the direct suppression ruling.)

The display or employment of firearms is an important issue. Weapons are most likely displayed before the frisk, rather than after, but they may be used before, during, or after based on behavior and what, if anything, is found. It is clear that a law enforcement officer's intentional discharge of a firearm to make a seizure is controlled by the dictates of applicable statutory law and the U.S. Supreme Court cases of *Tennessee v. Garner* 471 U.S. 1 (1985) and *Graham v. Connor*, 490 U.S. 386 (1989). The two cases are both Fourth Amendment "seizure" cases. The *Garner* case arose in the context of an arrest; *Graham* came from a "Terry stop." However, there is a great difference between a law enforcement officer pointing a firearm at or in the direction of an individual for tactically appropriate reasons and discharging that firearm. Among the differences is that **pointing a firearm is not a use of force**, despite the arguments sometimes made that it is. It is a threatened use of force used as a means of control. Compare the act of displaying or even pointing a firearm at a suspect with the definition of "force" in the first paragraph of this chapter. The assertion that drawing or pointing a firearm is a use of force is without merit and indicative of a lack of understanding of physics, the English language, and the law. (Remember the language quoted above from *Graham v. Connor*, in which the Court referred to "physical coercion" (force) or "the threat thereof," and thus made clear that they are not the same.)

It is a defense to the common law crime and tort of "assault" (essentially, placing a person in reasonable apprehension of receiving a "battery," an offensive or harmful touching) that the threatened force was legally justified. Logic indicates that if the "assault" is a tactically appropriate means of achieving a lawful objective, it is legally justified. If you have a reasonable basis for believing that the subject you are stopping is armed or may otherwise present a threat of death or great bodily harm to you, then it is irrational to deal with that person other than at gunpoint. Additionally, it may be necessary to hold persons at gunpoint in additional circumstances, for example, until sufficient police personnel are available to make it possible to interact with the persons with reasonable safety. Remember, we must create and display a recognizable advantage to minimize the potential for successful resistance. It is better to display (threaten) the potential use of such force and not need it than to refrain from such a display and allow a situation to deteriorate to the point that force must be used. Obviously, if you are attacked, you may use such force, up to and including force likely to cause death or great bodily harm, if that force is an "objectively reasonable" means of protecting yourself or another or arresting the offender for the attack.

As in all legal issues, your department's legal advisor should be part of the team responsible for drafting the policy to be followed. Any legal issue that affects a police department's operations must be examined and validated by the attorney responsible for the department's legal advice, along with the other subject matter experts whose knowledge is critical input. The authors have encountered articles and opinions on legal issues written by non-attorneys (and, to our frustration, some by attorneys) that are severely flawed in their research, analysis, and conclusions.

The Concept of Control

Reflecting more and more upon the issue of force has brought us to an understanding that its perspective ought to be more of a methodology than a concluding consequence. In other words, force is just an aspect of a much larger perspective of the interactive process between the officer and others.

At no other time in our occupational history have the role and responsibilities of the police had higher-profile public attention. This circumstance has revealed on-going friction between the police and some of the public. Most of this attention has been concentrated on the utilization of force. Much of the friction is the result of ignorance of the law. Some of it is the result of deliberate misstatements of the law, driven by mindsets and agendas that place the well-being of offenders on a par with that of officers and the victims of the offenders.

Although similar claims have been made about law enforcement in the past, and some were valid, the recent incidents and attention have revealed widely differing views across the country and among various populations. In order to improve the progress toward real crime prevention, communication about use of force must be addressed and improved.

Definition

Our research shows us that law enforcement agencies have often failed in even defining force. As a result, there is a lack of understanding and communication about whether we are using force properly. In fact, actually defining force is unusual and far too often made without a valid foundation. Far too many agencies continue to sidestep the core issue, allowing the term *force* to remain undefined, poorly defined, or misunderstood.

Evolution

Our research efforts for this revision have brought us to the conclusion that the understanding of what force is, from the lack of clarity in its definition to imprecise applications of any particular definition, is clearly inadequate.

In recent years, force has gone from being **a** means of individual control to being perceived by the public as **the** means! Although force is seldom utilized, it has overwhelmed public perception of our thoughts and our deeds. We as a profession have been shamefully passive in the pursuit of educating the policed, and thus gaining their support and cooperation.

Undoubtedly, *the preferred outcome of any contact between the police and policed is reasoned and rational control.* Compliance with the lawful authority of officers is the rational means of having such reasoned control. Control as a concept is not new or innovative, and it has stood the test of time. Naturally, we must include the public into our enforcement equation. It is that essential first step in providing the ideal interactive process between peace officers and the public with a well-understood program.

7   Bases for Interaction

If anything positive could or should come from the crisis in police/community relations over the last few years, it is the recognized need for greater dialog and a presumptive reduction in the distance evolving between the parties. Effective crime prevention is much more difficult when the communication is lacking.

To garner universal understanding of the challenges and circumstances within any given community, we must unite to enhance the mutual understanding of the roles and responsibilities of each for greater service and safety. We strongly believe that crime can and should be prevented and that many factors underlying criminality can be influenced by police. We believe the following:

- **Everyone, no matter what age, position, or capacity, can and must take individual action to stop crime.**
- **Partnerships that actually involve the local community and its residents are key to preventing crime.**
- **Prevention is the most cost-effective alternative to the ravages of crime to individuals, neighborhoods, and communities.**
- **Crime prevention action should be grounded in research and tested approaches and aided by evaluation.**

The core goal of our efforts is to provide greater understanding and cooperation between the police and the policed through understanding, education, and cooperation. Addressing the needs, safety, and security of all is the essence of effective economics and life. We are providing sound, research-based legal and tactical concepts as part of the basis for these steps. There must also be reliable and validated data collection and analysis as to the conduct of officers and the efficacy of the actions taken. A large portion of the negative-discourse about policing is a result of poor or non-existent collection and analysis of data, resulting in perpetuating myths about police misconduct. If we do not take the opportunity to correct the resulting message, we will likewise be culpable in the resulting damage to the profession and society.

The comprehensive *Forward Through Ferguson* report addresses many perceived issues. Just as we assert, one of the most important issues is the lack of communication between the police and the rest of the community, resulting in not merely differing, but often incompatible, goals that are not understood by the two parties. The report called for one trait to act as the core for every effort—"a culture of trying." The structural circumstances and flaws of that region contributed to a perception that the police were part of the problem. More realistically, this perception of the police was a symptom of other structural problems. The long-term resentment of the entire structure of local government created a circumstance in which the intentional falsehoods about the assault on Officer Wilson and the subsequent death of Michael Brown were considered plausible to a large portion of the community. Part of the solution must be to "try"—to be part of improving the community by the use of enforcement tools that are uniquely available to the police as part of their contribution to the community. We must get out and be part of the community and ensure that we are seen as such. We must also communicate the legitimacy of enforcement activities; the failure to do so has resulted in being perceived as an illegitimate oppressor.

As Professor George E. Woodberry once said, "Defeat is not the worst of failures. Not to have tried is the true failure." There are very real impediments to the efforts to improve communication, but we must as a profession do our best to do so. The current situation in which there is utterly inadequate understanding is not good for any member of society, or for society as a whole. To try includes the individual and the institution in the plan to at least initiate the effort. We must also recognize that the interaction sought is the means to our mission of community tranquility.

The legacy of the Supreme Court's *Terry v. Ohio* decision almost 50 years ago has presented an intersection of precedent and purpose. The decision also reflects some of the very same tensions between the police and the policed with regard to community well-being and the path to take in order to achieve that goal that we see today. Astute practitioners will probably conclude that we as a profession have failed to ensure that our efforts are seen as legitimate, a conclusion supported by the return of some of the same assertions about the police as were made at the earlier time. This text is designed to address both the technical standards of "stop and frisk" and the inadequate communication about how this practice is a legitimate tool of community policing.

To enhance and clarify the mutual learning effort, we will explain the sequential interplay of officers and community members as the interaction moves from a consensual contact to increasing levels of intrusion. Each of the important words specific to the phase headings carry with them critical components we all should strive to support.

Social (or Consensual) Contact

First, more time and effort must be spent *walking and talking*, and less on *riding and hiding*. We have sworn to protect and serve an entire community, not just part of the community. It's a valuable strategy to get to know as many community members as possible. This activity is one built upon the mutual interests of both parties.

We must recognize that positive communication is a learning process, with the responsibility for performance being placed squarely and initially on the shoulders of peace officers. They must become the catalyst for progress by commencing greater interaction and exchange with all community members. Peace officers must remain part of the society, not apart from it.

Personal Interest

Every officer must have an individualized interest in the society that they have sworn to serve and protect. So, too, every community member must understand the importance of their involvement in the community.

Concerned Communication

When the public recognizes the role they play in the process of improving their community by becoming informed consumers of law enforcement services, they are taking direct steps toward that improvement. Who better to provide the necessary understanding than the peace officers in that community?

Individual Independence

Finally, the uniqueness of our core value of freedom clearly depends upon the knowledge that our rights and responsibilities are preserved and protected by those sworn to do so. The existence of a peaceful environment must be preserved by crime prevention. It is more about developing rapport than a reputation.

Strategic Control—Making a Stop

If an officer develops a *reasonable suspicion of criminal activity* and is able to articulate it appropriately, then an investigative stop, by whatever name, has long been accepted as a legitimate and important part of an officer's enforcement repertoire.

Professional Perception and Articulation

Now, the officer's expertise justifies an enforcement activity that is no longer just social in nature. As we have learned, the individual **MUST** submit to the officer's reasonable investigative detention. By sharing this information with the policed, the activity would be less the subject of ignorant commentary and thus less likely to meet with resistance.

We all benefit by this example of an *active crime suppression* program by someone society has selected and trained to exercise this legitimate authority.

Community concern should prompt the professional officer to do their duty, to act inquisitively when "things don't look right," and to utilize their enforcement expertise. "Seeing and saying" reflects a sophistication that comes with experience and training.

Reasonable Suspicion

The basis for the officer's response is entirely based upon legal precedent. If he or she is able to articulate reasonably that the subject is acting in a way that is criminally related, a significant part of the strategy for community crime prevention is to initiate a "stop" of the individual as allowed by law. Factors that officers should consider when deciding to make a stop include, but may not be limited to:

1. Subject appearance—Does this person generally fit the description of a suspect in a known offense? Does this person fit your knowledge of persons generally encountered in this area? Are this person's clothes consistent with the weather and other conditions?
2. The subject's actions—Does this person appear to be fleeing? Is his or her behavior consistent with your knowledge of criminal activity? If so, what activity and behavior? Is he or she with others who by these factors also appear suspicious? Were conversations overheard which contributed to your suspicions?
3. Prior knowledge of the person—Does he or she have an arrest or conviction record, or does other credible information connect him or her to criminal offenses? If so, does that information relate to offenses similar to the one believed to have occurred, or which is suspected to be about to occur? What other knowledge do you have about this person?
4. Demeanor during the contact—If the subject responded to questions during the contact, what was the nature of his or her answers? Were they evasive, suspicious on their own, or incriminating? What sort of non-verbal communication was displayed during the encounter?
5. Area of the stop—Is the subject near the area of a known crime soon after it occurred? Is the area known for high levels of criminal activity? Do the subject's actions or appearance match a type of crime for which the area is known?
6. Time of day—Is it unusual for people to be in the area at this time? Is it a time of day during which a certain type of crime is occurring, according to your knowledge or department intelligence?
7. Law enforcement training and experience (including personal and professional knowledge of the area)—Do this subject's appearance and behavior resemble a pattern followed in particular offenses? How does this subject's behavior compare to typical behavior in this particular area under similar conditions?

8. Law enforcement purpose—Are you investigating a specific crime, type of crime, or pattern of criminal activity? What type of crime?
9. Source of information—What is the basis for your suspicions? If part of the basis is information supplied by another person, what do you know about this person? Is he or she a criminal informant, a witness, or a crime victim? How credible is this person? Has he or she supplied reliable information in the past? How did this person obtain this information? Can you corroborate this information? (This is a component of the analysis in which the officer's knowledge of the community members may be of vital importance.)

Temporary Detention

Importantly, for a "reasonable" amount of time the officer has the right and the responsibility to investigate suspicions in an attempt to confirm or dispel those suspicions. During this time the individual is not free to leave and subject to the officer's control. That control may be at as low a level as mere presence (which is not a use of force) or may involve the use of physical control options such as the Hand Control Position, applying the actual Hand Control Technique, the use of handcuffs, etc. Whatever force you find necessary to use, you must be able to justify by description of the observations/perceptions that caused that to be an "objectively reasonable" decision. At this point there may also be a basis upon which to "frisk" the detained person. The justification for a "stop" does not automatically justify a "frisk."

A "frisk" is a limited protective "search" for concealed weapons or dangerous instruments that may be used to attack the officer or another person. An example of a statute pertaining to the "frisk" component of *Terry* is included below. That statute must also be construed in a manner consistent with the *Terry* decision and later cases. The statute states:

> When a peace officer has stopped a person for temporary questioning pursuant to Section 107–14 of this Code and reasonably suspects that he or another person is in danger of attack, he may search the person for weapons. If the officer discovers a weapon, he may take it until the completion of questioning, at which time he shall either return the weapon, if legally possessed, or arrest the person so questioned.

You must remember that "search" as used in the statute is not the same kind of search made in an arrest situation or pursuant to a warrant. It is a "frisk," which is generally limited to a patdown of the outer garments of the person stopped. You may perform such a frisk at any time that the reasonable suspicion arises that you or another person are in danger of attack. The reasonable suspicion that justifies a frisk is more than a mere hunch but less than "probable cause." If a reasonably cautious officer, under the circumstances, would believe that he or she or others in the area of the stop are in danger because the person stopped might be in possession of a weapon, then a frisk is justified. The same considerations mentioned earlier, in the material introducing the factors that may be applicable to the stop decision, apply when making a decision about whether or not a frisk is appropriate.

Additionally, **a frisk is not justified just because a stop is justified; this is a second, separate decision.** The analysis and decision may actually be made at the same time and include some of the same factors, depending on the situation that led to the stop. Of particular importance is the nature of the crime suspected or being investigated; the greater the potential for violence directed at officers as indicated by the crime, the greater the likelihood that a frisk will be appropriate. W. LaFave, *Search and Seizure: A Treatise on the Fourth Amendment*, 5th ed. (West, St. Paul, 2012) § 9.6a.

Some factors that should be considered include, but are not limited to:

1. **The person's appearance**—Is he or she wearing clothing or carrying items that are capable of concealing a weapon? Do the clothes bulge in a manner that is suggestive of a concealed weapon? Consider the ways you carry concealed weapons and your experience about how choice of clothes and weapons affect each other.
2. **The person's actions**—Was a furtive movement consistent with checking or hiding a weapon made as your presence was noticed or you approached? This great description is from *Bland v. Commonwealth*, 66 Va. App. 405, 410 (2016): (Appellant "looked in [their] direction" then "patted his front right pocket, his right rear pocket, and then pulled [his] shirt down . . . on [the right] side." Officer Butler understood this action as being consistent with the type of movements in which one conducting a "weapons check" would engage. Butler characterized a "weapons check" as the efforts of an armed person "to make sure [their weapon] is still there.") Is the person displaying signs of extreme nervousness? Are his or her words or actions threatening?
3. **Prior knowledge of the person**—Does this person have a reputation for being unlawfully armed, committing assaults on police officers, or other violent behavior? (If one is able to identify the subject prior to approaching, and check his or her name in any local dispatch system, then any prior history discovered or reported to the officer would satisfy this factor and improve safety.)
4. **Location**—Is this a high-crime area, especially one known for crimes that carry an increased risk of violent resistance to your actions? Is this area sufficiently isolated or hostile to law enforcement officers that you are unlikely to receive help if attacked? **(In which case, why would you make the stop without sufficient officer presence?)**
5. **Time of day**—Is this a nighttime or other low-light encounter? Does that improve the ability of the person to assault you?
6. **Law enforcement purpose**—Do your suspicions about this person relate to a violent, armed, or other serious offense that may raise the potential danger to you?

7. **Companions**—Have you stopped a number of persons at once? **(Why? Stops of more than one person should be avoided or delayed until enough backup officers are present.)** Has a frisk of one of these persons produced a weapon?

Again, this is not necessarily a complete list; if you have a better or more complete set of criteria upon which to base your decisions, use it.

Once again, a frisk is a limited search for purposes of protection only, based on reasonable suspicion (which is less than probable cause) that the person might be armed. *Ybarra v. Illinois*, 444 U.S. 85 (1979). Remember that as the law with regard to private citizens being armed in public has shifted in favor of such being lawful in an increasing number of states, you will encounter more people who rely upon such statutes. Merely being armed in public is not a basis for a "Terry stop." Of course, if they are carrying a properly concealed handgun, it is unlikely that you will have complaints that draw your attention to any such person.

Although the mere possession of a concealed or openly carried firearm where that would generally be lawful is not a basis for a "Terry stop," the circumstances are much different when a person is stopped for some other lawful reason and believed to be armed. In general, such a frisk is lawfully permitted, as the reasoning of *Terry* and its immediate progeny, such as *Adams v. Williams*, 407 U.S. 143 (1972), concludes that a person who is armed is dangerous. This conclusion does not vary by whether or not the person is or may be lawfully armed. There is only one case of which the authors are aware that has come to a contrary conclusion. *State v. Cruz*, 195 Wn. App. 120 (as modified and reconsideration denied, Sept. 22 2016), a case in which discretionary review by the Washington Supreme Court has been granted as of March 30, 2017. *United States v. Robinson*, 846 F. 3d 694 (*en banc*, 2017) provides a good discussion of the general rule.

The purpose of the frisk is not to discover evidence, but for the protection of the officer; if it goes past the point necessary for the protection of the officer, then it is no longer valid under the reasoning of the *Terry* case, and anything discovered will be suppressed. *Minnesota v. Dickerson*, 508 U.S. 366, 373 (1993). If the person is carrying an object that can be separated from the person, such as a purse or briefcase, then the items should be placed in a secure location (such as the squad car) for the duration of the stop. Generally, such an item should only be examined as part of the frisk if you have reason to believe that this item is the location of a weapon. If you don't have such a reason, the examination of this item may be difficult to justify, since the point of this action is protection; it is not a search based on probable cause. Most of the time, handcuffing will not be considered proper by the courts, but it may be legally sound if the basis for doing so is properly articulated. Once the frisk is complete, the handcuffs must be removed unless the individual is now to be arrested as a result of items found during the frisk, or you can articulate the safety-based reason for not doing so. W. LaFave, *Search and Seizure: A Treatise on the Fourth Amendment*, 5th ed. (West, St. Paul, 2012) § 9.2d.

Once the subject has been tactically approached and controlled (to be presented later), start the frisk on that part of the person's clothing most likely to be able to conceal a weapon or dangerous instrument. The frisk is limited to a patdown of the outer garments, unless:

1. The outer clothing is too bulky to allow you to determine if a weapon is concealed underneath, in which case outer clothing such as coats may be opened to allow a direct frisk of the inner clothing (shirts, trousers, etc.), or
2. You have a reasonable belief, based on reliable information or your own knowledge and observations that a weapon is concealed in a particular location on the person, such as a pocket, waistband, or sleeve. In this event, you may reach directly into the suspected area. This is an unusual procedure, and you must again be prepared to cite the precise factors that lead you to act in this manner instead of following a normal patdown procedure.

Adams v. Williams, 407 U.S. 143 (1972)

You may also frisk or secure any areas within the detained person's immediate reach if you reasonably suspect that such areas might contain a weapon. If, when conducting a frisk, you feel an object that you reasonably believe is a weapon, you may reach directly into that area of the person's clothing and remove the item.

If the item is a weapon, secure the weapon away from the person for the duration of the encounter, then determine whether or not their possession of the weapon is lawful. If the item, once seen, may be seized on another basis (such as being evidence, proceeds, or instruments of a crime), then it should be seized and considered in determining whether or not there is probable cause to arrest the person. If removal of the item reveals another object that is subject to seizure, you can seize this second item and proceed as described above. Of course, if during the stop you develop the basis to make a full-custody arrest of the person based on probable cause, you will be entitled to make a complete search, and any items found will be properly seizable as evidence.

If while conducting a frisk, you encounter an item that you do not believe to be a weapon, but do believe to be otherwise seizable, you cannot on the basis of the legal authority for the frisk take further steps to examine the object, except under the limited circumstances described in *Minnesota v. Dickerson*, 508 U.S. 366 (1993). *Sibron v. New York*, 392 U.S. 40, 65–66 (1968). The United States Supreme Court has explained the limits of the frisk for weapons in *Dickerson*; this case is so important to understand that we examine it in greater detail. In this case, two Minneapolis police officers made a proper investigative stop, with a proper frisk, of a man (Dickerson) seen leaving a known crack house. The officer who conducted the frisk encountered an object in one of Dickerson's pockets. After manipulating the object with his fingers, the officer concluded that it felt like crack cocaine packaged in cellophane, and he retrieved the package. On appeal, the Court explained the limits of a frisk in this manner:

> If a police officer lawfully pats down a suspect's outer clothing and feels an object whose contour or mass makes its identity immediately apparent, there has been no invasion of the suspect's privacy beyond that authorized by the officer's search for weapons; if the object is contraband, its warrantless seizure would be justified.
>
> *Minnesota v. Dickerson*, 508 U.S. 366, 375–376 (1993)
> (analogizing to the "plain-view" doctrine)

Applying that principle to the facts of the case, the Court held that this manipulation of the object went beyond the permissible scope of the frisk, because the officer made his determination only after " 'squeezing, sliding and otherwise manipulating the contents of the defendant's pocket'—a pocket which the officer already knew contained no weapon." 508 U.S. 366 at 378. "Here, the officer's continued exploration of respondent's pocket after having concluded that it contained no weapon was unrelated to '[t]he sole justification of the search [under Terry:] the protection of the police officer and others nearby.'" 508 U.S. 366 at 378 (citing *Terry*). The legal effect of this decision is to make it clear that once officer safety needs have been met, by determining whether or not the person you have stopped is armed, there is no justification for examining another object encountered unless you can tell immediately, without any examination greater than that already made, that the object is contraband.

The practical effect is to strictly limit the scope of the examination of objects discovered during a frisk. It will be virtually impossible to seize anything wrapped in a manner similar to that described in the *Dickerson* case, since the contents, not the wrapping, is the contraband; probable cause to believe that the contents are contraband will almost never exist without a visual examination. That visual examination will not be possible in most cases, because probable cause must exist **before** the object can be retrieved and examined. The Court recognized "that officers will less often be able to justify seizures of unseen contraband" as a result of a protective frisk, but properly stated that "the Fourth Amendment's requirement that the officer have probable cause to believe that the item is contraband before seizing it protects against excessively speculative seizures." 508 U.S. 366 at 376.

We discussed this decision with several officers and trainers; we could think of very few contraband objects that could be sufficiently identified within the limitations of this case. Remember, probable cause to believe that the object is contraband must be formed during the initial frisk, using only techniques that will disclose a weapon, not more invasive techniques. One possible response that might work for some assignments is to design a program that focuses on training officers to recognize the feel of the form of contraband that their assignment is focused on. A properly designed and documented training program may allow officers to learn how to recognize certain other objects as contraband. For example, officers working in an area with certain types of drug activity may be able to learn to recognize some kinds of drug paraphernalia and properly seize it. This training, done in a manner similar to training in recognition of impaired drivers, with increased "hands-on" time, should be sufficient to provide a foundation for admission of such evidence in court. Consulting with your department's attorney and local prosecutor while developing the training will maximize your odds of success. **A more practical thought is this: if you have to risk making a mistake in a situation like this, err in favor of your own safety. No case is worth your life.**

If the frisk does not disclose a weapon or other seizable item, you may now continue the investigation of the circumstances, but of course you can't assume that there is now no possibility of attack. Remember that the reasonableness of the length of the detention will depend on the circumstances you encounter. W. LaFave, *Search and Seizure: A Treatise on the Fourth Amendment*, 5th ed. (West, St. Paul, 2012) § 9.2f. If the person is not arrested after the encounter, any items secured during the encounter are to be returned; the return should be done in a manner consistent with your safety.

Systemic Control—an Arrest

Finally, the officer may make an arrest as a result of the investigative inquiry or independently developed probable cause identifying that individual and connecting him or her to a criminal act. Although an arrest is the most serious stage in the process, it is not a conclusion; it is a commencement of an adversarial setting based upon fairness, impartiality, and presumed innocence.

Probable Cause

Now the articulable facts must be supportive of the concept of "probable cause"; that is, that it is more probable than not that an offense was committed and more probable than not by this person or persons, rather than that of a "reasonable suspicion." The individual's seizure, potential search, and actual detention are each structured by the judicial system and subject to its demands for truth and facts.

Judicial Oversight

Each accused individual will have the ability to go before a court and enter a plea as to the nature of the criminal accusation; bail and other pre-trial matters such as the right to counsel will be considered, all consistent with legal requirements.

Potential Confinement

Following the consideration of pre-trial steps by judicial authority, incarceration or other restrictions could occur for a period of time before trial or other resolution of the enforcement activity.

Evolving Toward the Future

Clearly, the first stage in the interactive process of community crime prevention places officers in the position of initiation. Their personal and/or professional interest is conveyed to members of the population whose rights and other interests they protect. Departments should encourage these interactions as a part of duty, with the dual goals of increased informational exchange and communal cooperation and decreased distancing.

Once again, society's protectors are in the best position to begin the process, and the whole community benefits from the product. This "new normal" should allow for measured and mutually cooperative commitment. The common goal sought is a safer and more secure population.

Section III

Police Strategy and Tactics

8 Fundamentals of Policing

Face-to-face interaction between an officer and an individual is a core concept of community policing and crime prevention. Although a critical component for the desired goal, it is an occurrence that has apparently decreased in frequency over the years. Such an effort could evolve from some form of inquiry free of any suspicious circumstances.

Neither the Constitution nor any other legal source prohibits you from being curious about things you see or the interests you may have. Refer back to the more detailed attention paid to this concept and the *Royer* case previously.

We suggest that the number of these contacts be maximized, regardless of the shift or the environment. The more casual contact you have with as many individuals as possible, the more you "sell" yourself, your agency, and the crime prevention mission. Ideally, theses interactions should be reported and/or recorded and tabulated for future reference and research.

Remember, as skilled as we may be due to education, training, and experience, we can never totally predict the actions or responses within an officer/subject interaction. This is certainly the case relative to an officer and individual contact. Therefore, in our effort to maximize control and officer safety, our approach toward the individual encounter should be founded upon tactics that are consistent with overall safety and security.

Officer's Protective Stance

Field analysis has indicated that the traditional "protective stance" best exhibits the essential traits of protective positioning, calculated caution, and situational safety and should be incorporated through patterns of professional practice until it becomes a conditioned response.

Lower Torso

The foundation of the "stance" is balance (see Figure 8.1). Balance is best achieved by the officer assuming a solid base, conscious of the body's center of gravity. The officer's weak or off foot is forward, pointed toward the subject. The officer's strong or primary foot should be about a shoulder width behind

Figure 8.1 Alert Stance

the weak foot at an angle of 45 to 90 degrees. This foot positioning allows the officer the best options potentially relative to balance, mobility, leverage, and strength utilization.

Upper Torso

The officer's upper torso should also contribute to safety, as well as the potential for the initiation of effective countermeasure controls. This capacity is best realized by the officer keeping his or her elbows close to the body, with his or her hands maintained at least above the waist.

Body Clock/Risk Radius

If we were standing above the subject, looking down, we could identify risk potential by a numerical clock-like reference and the darker shading in the area of increased risk (Figure 8.2). Danger increases as we gain closer proximity to the individual, and likewise, greater distancing provides increasing degrees of risk reduction, also shown by the variation in shading.

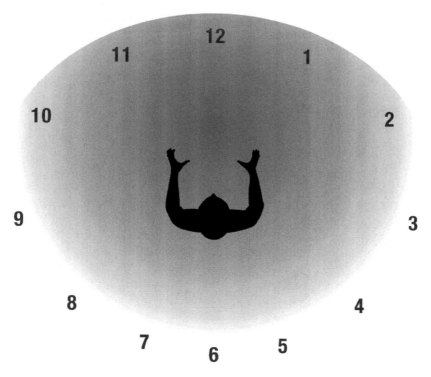

Figure 8.2 Risk Radius

As a result of additional tactical research, we have learned that 6 o'clock, or the rear position, represents the greatest vulnerability to the individual, and therefore offers the potential for officer superiority. So too, as we move from the rear to the front of the body, or 12 o'clock, we are losing a major tactical advantage and presumably a reduction in officer safety and strategic stance. Such placement should be avoided from initiation to completion of any eventual encounter.

Positioning

The "protective stance" places the officer(s) at a relatively safe distance (5–8 feet) to the front/side of the subject upon initial contact. From this position, the risk of being punched or kicked by the citizen can be somewhat reduced, and the individual's actions may be more easily detected or deflected. The contact itself should be perceived as a positive experience by the subject and should also be an expression of the officer's skill in deploying the **Encounter Formula (Recognizable Advantage for the Officer/Recognizable Disadvantage for the Subject)**.

The officer should avoid being distracted by the subject's eyes during the encounter, thus preventing the potential for distractions such as fakes, hostile expressions, etc., and should place primary sight concentration on the subject's upper chest area. This positioning and perception should keep the subject's entire body within either the officer's primary or peripheral view. Always make sure that the subject's hands are constantly and clearly visible. Therefore, if the subject's actions were to change, the officer could better perceive the risks presented and begin to initiate proper countermeasures to gain compliance and control.

Communication/Control Officer Approach and Positioning

Ideally with each contact, the principle of **Tactical Transition (Ability of the Officer to Respond Tactically to the Degree of Noncompliance from the Subject)** and the concept of the **Encounter Formula** are integrated into a conditioned performance.

Generally, two officers approach an individual who will be at the apex of a triangle, allowing them to remain to the front/sides of the subject (Figure 8.3). It is probable that most truly "social" contacts will not involve two officers unless they are already engaged in an activity at which two or more officers are already present and the contact is incidental to that, or both wish to learn information from a potential witness, or some other relatively low-profile activity. If in fact you perceive a need to have a second officer present, one should seriously consider whether there are other factors that make this encounter something that is suspicion based and change their approach accordingly.

As a result of this dual positioning, the subject will most commonly begin to verbally or visually address one of the officers. Dialogue may also be initiated by one of the officers during the approach as part of a tactical plan.

Figure 8.3 Enhanced Perspective

In either case, the officer who is first to establish communication with the subject becomes the **Communication Officer**, continuing to maintain the subject's attention, providing an on-going avenue for present or potential verbal direction to the subject and/or a source of information reception.

The support officer now assumes an enhanced, strategic position for potential countermeasure controlling techniques from the front/side, side, side/rear, or rear of the subject, thus becoming the **Control Officer**. This officer also retains information and perceives subject actions in a supplemental but silent sense, unless providing some form of communication to the Communication Officer. The Control Officer can now view the subject from an enhanced perspective and position in reference to potential controlling efforts.

If the subject were to change communicative direction to the opposite officer, **Tactical Transition** would call for each of the officers to switch their

Communication and **Control** roles, so as to continue to maximize the tactical advantage for both officers.

Note: The authors believe that if such interaction were to result in an offense report, it is inconsistent with a social contact and probably indicates enforcement intention and results. However, as another example of transition, it may be that the interaction started as something in the nature of a social contact but evolved due to officer perceptions, subject actions, and other factors. Officers must perceive and communicate that transition just as they must do so with regard to tactics. Officers should prepare a report or other record devoted to the fact of the contact and any information obtained.

If what began as a consensual contact were to transition to a "stop," or if the encounter were to begin at that stage, the officer(s) need to consider higher levels of control as discussed previously. Here, we discuss the application of temporary restraints, also known as handcuffs.

Restraints

Under limited circumstances, a subject could be handcuffed prior to the initiation of a frisk. Perhaps, facts perceived during the frisking process will indicate a need to increase the level of control imposed on the subject. Such perceptions could reveal probable cause for an arrest, and prompt handcuffing is the tactical choice for matters of threat prevention, control, etc.

Due to the variance encountered within the interactive process, we have included both dual officer application and removal procedures and single officer application and removal techniques. In this regard, we subscribe to the principles of policing mentioned earlier and the foundation of the **Encounter Formula** as a key to officer safety, thus emphasizing the dual officer procedures as being the better choice.

Dual Officer Application

The safety of both officers is maximized by the directed de-stabilization of the subject along with a continuous observation of the individual by both officers from a proper position while in the **Alert Stance** as noted earlier in the text.

The subject is directed to slowly rotate completely around, eventually stopping with his back to the officers, with both hands fully extended to his side, with the palms to the rear. Next, he is directed to bend at the waist, spread his feet wide apart, keep his head up, and to bring both hands back to the officers with the palms out and the thumbs directed upward.

Both officers now simultaneously make contact with the subject's hand corresponding to the officer's position, with each officer initiating the **Hand Control Position** (Figure 8.4) on the subject's corresponding hand. The graphic shows four steps in initiating and obtaining the Hand Control Position.

One of the controlling officers now removes his handcuffs from the case with his free hand. The officer's hand is placed in the center portion of the

Hand Control
POSITION

- static
- painless

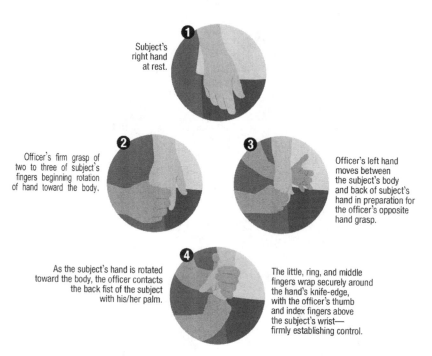

❶ Subject's right hand at rest.

❷ Officer's firm grasp of two to three of subject's fingers beginning rotation of hand toward the body.

❸ Officer's left hand moves between the subject's body and back of subject's hand in preparation for the officer's opposite hand grasp.

❹ As the subject's hand is rotated toward the body, the officer contacts the back fist of the subject with his/her palm.

The little, ring, and middle fingers wrap securely around the hand's knife-edge, with the officer's thumb and index fingers above the subject's wrist— firmly establishing control.

Figure 8.4 Hand Control Position

handcuffs for greater stability as he places the handcuff on the subject's controlled wrist. The support officer now moves the subject's other wrist into position, where it now can be handcuffed. Once the handcuffs are applied to both wrists, they are checked for proper application and double-locked.

Final application of the handcuffs should be positioned so that the double bar is up, the single bar is down, and the lock port opening is toward the subject. This overall handcuff placement not only reduces the "pick" potential of the handcuffs by the subject or others but aids in the eventual removal of the handcuffs by the officer.

Note: If at any time during the handcuffing process the subject were to become non-compliant, one or both officers could make the immediate **Tactical Transition** from the **Hand Control Position** to the **Hand Control Technique** (Figure 8.5) by increasing the tension, pressure, and redirection.

Hand Control
TECHNIQUE

- **dynamic**
- **painful**

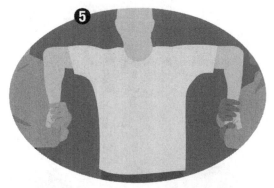

If either or both of officers perceive the subject as Resistant (Active),
they immediately enhance the controlled hand's rotation toward the body
while the subject's elbow moves upward resulting in extreme tension.

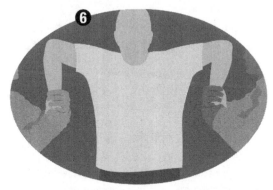

Both officers continue to direct the subject's elbow upward while rotating the controlled hand
until compliance is achieved. At that point the individual can be directed into a variety of positions:
standing, kneeling, and prone; readied for common enforcement activities
like immobilization, frisking, handcuffing, etc.

Figure 8.5　Hand Control Technique

Dual Officer Removal

Field analysis has shown that significant risks can arise when handcuffs are
removed from the subject. Once the decision is made to remove the handcuffs
from the subject, he is again directed into a position of de-stabilization, and
the **Hand Control Position** is initiated on the subject by both officers.

One officer removes the handcuff from the wrist controlled by the remaining support officer. This officer now releases the handcuff on the wrist that he controls. During this period, the officer may desire to stabilize the handcuff with his thumb during the unlocking process.

The officer can now return his handcuff key to his person as he continues to control the subject's hand and arm via the **Hand Control Position**. The officer now removes the handcuff with his free hand. Once the handcuff is removed and replaced in the handcuff case, and both officers acknowledge the response, the subject is simultaneously released by each officer from the **Hand Control Position**.

Single Officer Application

It is suggested that only under exigent circumstances should a single officer apply handcuffs. Unfortunately, we must recognize that a large percentage of our enforcement encounters place the officer in a one-to-one contact ratio. **We must remember the increased risk inherent in such an encounter and work to make this situation the exception rather than the rule.**

Once again, the subject is initially visually examined and then directed into a de-stabilized position with his back to the officer. At this point, two options are presented.

Option 1

The subject is directed to bring both hands to the rear with the palms together. The subject is then told to interlock his fingers. He is then directed to rotate both of his hands in unison with the thumbs positioned upward.

The officer now initiates the **Hand Control Position** on the subject's right hand with his left hand. The officer now places the handcuff on the subject's controlled wrist. The officer now directs the subject to release his interlocked left hand from his controlling right hand and to return his wrist back to the handcuffed wrist area, where it is subsequently handcuffed.

Note: During the application of the second handcuff is a common point at which serious non-compliance is initiated by non-compliant individuals.

Option 2

From the interlocked position noted earlier, the officer applies the first handcuff on the subject's controlled wrist. The subject is then directed to release his left hand from the interlocked position. The officer now establishes a firm grasp on the subject's left index and middle fingers, directing the fingers upward toward the subject's spine. While being restrained by this coercive method, the remaining handcuff is now applied on the subject's left wrist.

In both options, handcuffs are checked for proper application and double-locked by the officer. Again, if at any time during the handcuffing process the subject were to become non-compliant, the officer would initiate the **Tactical**

Transition by increasing tension, pressure, and repositioning via the **Hand Control Technique**.

Single Officer Removal

Again, it is suggested that only under limited circumstances should a single officer perform the handcuff removal process. If such conditions do occur, a single officer follows the same procedures outlined in the dual officer removal portion.

The officer initiates control of the de-stabilized subject via the **Hand Control Position** on the subject's right hand and releases the handcuff on the subject's non-controlled hand and wrist. The subject is directed to take this free hand and place it on top of his head, or away from his body, while the officer secures the remaining handcuff for potential removal.

During this process the officer should position his controlling thumb over the top strand of the positioned handcuff. The officer now releases the handcuff from the subject's controlled hand and wrist. Again, once the handcuff is released, the officer should replace the handcuff key on his person. Additionally, once the handcuff is removed, the officer should replace his handcuffs into the handcuff case while still maintaining the **Hand Control Position** on the subject.

On occasion the officer(s) may have to implement countermeasures against the subject that will result in the subject becoming kneeling or prone. Here too, the officer(s) must have tactics of restraint application consistent with such positioning. These tactics will be addressed in the following pages, consistent with the fundamental tactical skills already illustrated.

On occasion the individual may initiate non-compliance during the officer/subject interaction. Once again, if you have nothing more than a hunch, suspicion, etc. that is not supported by a "reasonable suspicion of a crime," then the subject can leave the scene on his or her own accord. But if the "reasonable suspicion of a crime" exists, or probable cause for an arrest can be supported, the officer should initiate countermeasures to impose control.

Non-compliant Subjects

Note: At this point, the encounter has almost certainly moved from an investigative detention ("Terry stop") to whatever your state law defines as "obstructing" your performance as a result of that non-compliance, and you are now making an arrest. You need to be aware, and do what you can to make the subject aware, that he or she is now under arrest. Further resistance at that point is possibly an additional crime, again depending on your state statutes. (Compare Washington RCW 9A.76.020 and 9A.76.040, which makes the above acts two crimes, with California PC § 148(a)(1).) Any assaultive conduct is of course yet another crime.

Under such circumstances, officers must be aware of the steps to a controlling position via **Tactical Transition** made available by the utilization of the **Hand Control Position** and the **Hand Control Technique**, previously detailed. Both of these inter-related procedures were adapted to policing to facilitate the imposition of officer control throughout such a confrontation. We have presented these procedures for both dual officer and single officer usage and with the concluding/controlling positional options of standing, kneeling, and prone.

Remember, once again, that the achievement of the **Encounter Formula** and its mandate of recognized advantage prompts the significance of the sequencing of the Dual Officer and Single Officer presentation that follow.

Dual Officer—Standing Position

In the event that the **Hand Control Position** fails to maintain the subject's compliance, the tactic can be transitioned into the **Hand Control Technique** via increased tension and movement. Ideally, both officers initiate such transition in a controlled manner until the subject is managed. Once compliance is achieved, the subject is directed and assisted to bring his hands and arms to the rear of his body by both officers, and handcuffs are appropriately applied. We advocate "cuff, then search." The proper application of handcuffs, while not completely securing the subject, does substantially reduce his ability to effectively resist, including the possibility of gaining access to weapons on his person and those of the officers.

Remember, the person's proximity to the weapons on or about the waist is still significant and should be the initiation point of the comprehensive search activity by both officers. If the searching process reveals material necessitating removal from the subject's possession, it should be secured on either officer's person. To the extent possible, the position on the officer's person should correspond to its location on the subject.

Note: The nature of the contraband, weapon, etc. must be considered and "made safe" as much as possible by the officer as part of properly securing it. So too, such a searching and securing process should remain consistent throughout each of the positions that are presented.

Dual Officer—Alternative Positions

Note: If at any time either officer feels that he may fail to maintain the noncompliant subject under control in the standing position, appropriate communication should be initiated between both officers, who in unison should direct and assist the subject to the ground. As noted, the following takedown technique presented allows the officers the option of a kneeling or prone subject positioning for a controlled conclusion.

Kneeling Position Transition

Both officers have initiated and properly applied the **Hand Control Technique** on the subject and have now directed the subject downward toward a kneeling position. As the subject responds to the directive, both officers must still maintain the maximized effective position of the subject's arm repositioning as necessary.

Once the subject has reached the ground with both knees, he is directed to cross his left ankle over the other, and to then sit back on his lower leg and ankles. At this point if compliance is achieved, both officers return to the rear of the subject if necessary and return to the **Hand Control Position** on the subject by reducing the tension and begin the handcuffing process. Once again, as long as compliance continues, the subject should be directed and assisted to his feet and the comprehensive search conducted accordingly.

Note: If such positioning does not result in compliance, the officers immediately direct the subject to the prone position, which is subsequently detailed.

Prone Position Transition

As mentioned previously, both officers continue to maintain the **Hand Control Technique** on the standing or kneeling non-compliant subject. Due to the subject's continued or increased degree of non-compliance, he is "grounded" for the greater control and safety that results from further decreased mobility.

The subject is directed to the prone position on the ground by both officers. During this phase of the process, each officer can gain directed control via the **Hand Control Technique**. Enhancing its effectiveness by pushing forward and down on the subject's elbow with a support hand may be appropriate.

Each officer now pivots around to the front of the subject's controlled arm, continuing to exert pain compliance via the **Hand Control Technique** and/ or by pulling it forward and downward with a support hand, until the prone position is achieved.

Once the subject is prone, the officers should continue to maintain the controlled arms in a position a minimum of 90 degrees from the subject's body. Both officers now assume a kneeling position, with the knee corresponding to the controlling hand, placed on the ground as the weight-bearing foundation. The officer's other knee should be placed above the subject's upper back area to provide positional containment and control of the subject.

Note: Such activity may prompt the officers to be stressed by the response, resulting in increased levels of adrenaline. The officers must ensure that their weight-bearing knee is in contact with the ground, so as not to place unnecessary pressure on the subject's back area. It is possible that in the course of overcoming the resistance that this protective step will be delayed, but officers must be as aware as possible of the risk and their placement, and address it as quickly as they can. Once the subject becomes compliant, the handcuffing process is initiated.

Once secured, and when tactically feasible, the subject should be rolled on his side, with the front of his body away from the participating officer, and a cursory search attempted. Remember the type of search is still prone to errors in terms of subject access to weapons, etc.

Subsequently, the officer should move around the head of the subject and now roll the individual on his remaining side. Again with the front of the subject's body away from the officer, a similar search is conducted. When tactically feasible, the subject should be assisted to his feet and made ready for transport.

Generally, this is most easily accomplished by the officer directing the subject to tuck his legs up under his body, and then with the assistance of another officer on the opposite side of the subject, assist him to his feet. Now standing, the subject should be given a comprehensive search in unison or in succession by the officers prior to transport. The nature and tactics noted previously should still apply for safety and security reasons.

Note: If for some reason the subject cannot be assisted to his feet, the subject should be moved to his side with his back to the controlling officer. He should be maintained in this position until removed by additional assistance or device (wheelchair, stretcher, etc.). Suspects on occasion have suffered unexpected medical problems due to the exertion of resistance, substance abuse, poor physical condition, and other factors, alone or in combination. If there is any perception of medial distress, such as difficulty breathing, medical assistance should be summoned immediately to respond on an emergent basis.

Note: Keep in mind that a thorough search has yet to be conducted on the subject, and such modification of the transport method may require adaptations in order to achieve a comprehensive examination.

Single Officer

Obviously, effectiveness and safety are jeopardized when an officer is one-to-one with a non-compliant subject, and such a situation should be avoided to the extent possible. However, reality may result in this ratio.

Standing Position

If the officer experiences a degree of non-compliance during the stop sequence, he should immediately initiate the **Tactical Transition** from the **Hand Control Position** to the **Hand Control Technique**. By this enhancement of tension and movement, the subject may be brought under control and compliance re-established.

Because the officer failed to fully apply the **Encounter Formula** initially, such response is now essential. It is further suggested that the officer direct the subject into either a kneeling or prone position, via the necessary transition, in order to initiate the handcuffing technique, which is subsequently presented.

Kneeling Position

The non-compliant subject is transitioned into the **Hand Control Technique** and potentially directed to his knees. Necessary movement to the side of the subject may be required in order to maximize the tension, prompting compliance. Once in the kneeling position, the subject is directed to bring the left ankle over the right ankle and sit back on the surface of the legs and ankles.

If compliance is achieved, the officer now applies the handcuff to the subject's controlled hand. The subject is then directed to bring his free hand back to the rear of his body, and the remaining handcuff is applied. The handcuffed subject is then assisted to his feet via the subject's earlier described leg tuck and the assistance of the officer present.

Note: However, if compliance is not perceived, the officer-directed course continues to the prone position.

Prone Position

If the officer feels the necessity of placing the non-compliant subject in a prone position, he has already initiated the **Tactical Transition** from the **Hand Control Position** to the **Hand Control Technique**. During this process, the officer pivots to the front of the subject while pulling downward on the subject's controlled arm in the area of the triceps muscle. The officer continues this downward directed pivot until the subject reaches the prone position.

Now the officer should place his non-weight-supporting knee and shin in the area of the subject's upper back and his weight-bearing knee onto the ground. If the subject has become compliant, the officer may choose to remain in this controlled position until additional assistance arrives (as suggested by the authors), or he may decide to initiate the handcuffing of the subject by applying the handcuff first to the controlled wrist and subsequently to the remaining free hand directed to the rear of the subject's body.

Once the handcuffs are applied, it is suggested that the officer continue to closely observe the subject for potential retrieval of weapons etc., until more assistance arrives in order to facilitate the previously mentioned standing search of the individual.

Note: Obviously, if the officer desires to continue the sequence of standing and searching the subject, the threat potential of the ratio and the unfulfilled nature of the Encounter Formula decreases the officer's safety. The unfortunate conditions prompting such a circumstance should be addressed with the goal of elimination.

9   Reporting/Recording

As with most other law enforcement activities, the proper reporting/recording of field contacts/interviews will help ensure the proper exercise of law enforcement authority and performance. The authors have also recognized, as have other interested and attentive professionals, that we are working in a new environment. We are now in a setting in which management must be able to **demonstrate** that our authority is being lawfully used, and that proper internal oversight is being applied. The popular narrative is knowingly false, but if we as a profession are not prepared to rebut the lies promptly, we will be stuck with them. Enormous damage has been done by the failure to address those lies, and we have to come from behind. Part of being able to do so is thorough knowledge and the data to support the improved communication.

You should also consider maintaining copies for your own files so that this information enhances your ability to recall the factors that lead you to conduct the field interview, what occurred during the encounter, and perhaps act as an incentive to initiate another opportunity.

Remember, these records are useful and important not only when the encounter leads to immediate arrest but even later as they lead to useful information for other investigations. One of the authors is familiar with an arrest and successful prosecution of a serial murderer that in part resulted from a very minor observation and contact that, when tied to other small pieces of information, led to the suspect.

Any time you're involved in a field interview, document the circumstances, identify the subject(s), and liberally record other facts and facets presented as soon as possible. Perhaps no other element of the investigative stop process is as critical as the officer's ability to articulate the relevancy of facts and the conclusions resulting from those facts in the light of experience in contact with a suspicious subject. You are unique, just as was Detective McFadden. Why not maximize what you have learned to do best?

The dictionary definition of *articulate* is "to speak or write in clear, expressive language." Articulation, then, is *the process of clearly enunciating your perceptions relative to a situation*. We would suggest that the reporting/recording element for such an activity be developed around the Field Interview Card, or other similar form known to most officers and agencies. As noted, this information should be recorded on a department form, such as an "F.I. card," your activity log, or a similar document, unless it results in an arrest.

If the encounter leads to an arrest, obviously, the facts and circumstances must be fully detailed in the arrest/incident report. If the field interview is based wholly or in part on information from an individual, you should attempt to obtain and record his or her identity and to verify the information before acting upon it.

Today we have the extension of the phenomenon by having the ability to "see and say" in a manner that generations before us never experienced. A photographic record of the encounter is essential. The camera is as valuable in the articulation and documentation process as your mind, voice, or memory—maybe more so. By its instantaneous and objective nature, it can act as a record for the experience, nature of the encounter, aspects of the environment, etc. It is even possible that subsequent analysis by others under different working conditions will reveal additional information of value.

Just remember that many facts can get "lost in the shuffle" of any institution, making a duplication useful. If your report writing software, or even standard word processing software, is properly configured, you will have the ability to save a copy of the original for yourself. Make use of it.

We have included a format that could be utilized for your efforts:

Date   Time   Location

IR# _____ Officer Personnel #(s) _____

Basis for contact _____

_____

[ ] Contact   [ ] Stop   [ ] Frisk   [ ] Restraint Application

Subject Name _____   Date of Birth _____

Address _____

_____

Height _____   Weight _____   Clothing _____

Description of Subject Activity (continue on back) _____

_____

Disposition (Control Utilization, etc.)_____

_____

Photograph Taken   [ ] Yes   [ ] No

We believe that such a form should be utilized on most individual contacts, but especially with those of a suspicious nature. This form should exhibit at least the same qualities of all police reports since so much is based upon the articulation of objective reasonableness in regard to the officer's responsive actions.

First, the information must be accurate in describing the factual details the officer observed and perceived. This information should flow in a logical manner and build upon the intuitive nature of the officer's experience and expertise. Next, the language should be simple and to the point. Lead the reader to the conclusions you drew upon for your suspicions of criminal conduct. Although you are a trained police officer, the hypothetical evaluator of your actions is a "reasonable person" absent your skills, so you have to show how and why you came to the conclusions at which you arrived. Remember how Detective McFadden expressed not only what he perceived but also what those observations meant to him and why. Finally, be complete and answer those same six questions that make up any report: who, what, when, where, why, and how.

> **Who**—Did you know the individual from a previous contact? Did he or she match a description of someone who was wanted in connection with a crime?
>
> **What**—What were the suspicious actions of the individual? What other factors prompted you to make contact with the individual?
>
> **When**—Was the contact following some criminal event? What time was it?
>
> **Where**—What was the exact location of your initial observations? Where did you first make contact with the subject? Where were certain forms of evidence located in reference to the contact?
>
> **Why**—Present a chronological picture of those activities of the subject that prompted the contact. Did the subject act more suspicious when he or she discovered you were watching?
>
> **How**—In what manner did you verbally and physically contact the subject? Did you use force to control the subject? Did you restrain the subject?

Remember, a photographic depiction can be of great assistance in the overall assessment of the reasonableness of your actions. Photographs can enhance a report narrative with actual visual descriptions of the surroundings, the subject's actions in reference to significant facets of the environment, etc. Body Worn Cameras (BWCs) are becoming more common among officers and agencies for a variety of reasons. Legal requirements and practice decisions about the use of BWCs can vary among states and communities. The knowledge and thoughts about best practices are evolving rapidly, so making specific recommendations is not feasible in this text. However, to the extent that footage from a BWC would also document such a "stop," this footage should be documented, reviewed, and stored in a manner similar to photos of such an event.

Supervisors too must be certain that a proper description of the circumstances is part of the incident report. Remember that your report has to "paint a picture" for people who weren't there. The better your report is, the more aggressively the prosecutor can proceed.

The quality of the reports provided to one of the authors have been a continued critical factor in charging and other decisions related to the direction of the case. So, too, in their mutual roles as peace officers, both authors constantly acted upon the recollection of previous experiences and references in applying their true police efficacy.

10 Model Policy

The authors determined that as we updated the text for this edition, we should provide a model policy that suggests some thoughts and directions for departments to consider in developing their procedures for conducting investigative detentions. (For our purposes, a "policy" is a mandate designed to influence and determine officer actions; "procedure" is the manner in which that mandate is implemented.) This is by necessity only a rough outline. The purchasers and readers of this text may be in any one of the 50 states, or even United States territories, each of which will have its own legal and social issues to consider. We have found that agencies around the country have widely varying degrees of specificity in their procedural provisions, and the writing styles may vary even more. We are not trying to tell agencies how to write, but suggesting how to provide information that maximizes success and minimizes liability and social strife.

We are very much dedicated to having all parts of the management team conducting research and contributing their relevant knowledge to all aspects of law enforcement operations. Accordingly, it is our expectation that the actual policy to be implemented will include communication among the legal staff and patrol procedures/tactics instructors. It is no secret that sometimes there are problems in communication among these parties. In order to assist with overcoming that issue, we would like to offer some thoughts for your consideration, in the hope that once you know what kind of attributes the other parties have, you can do a better job of communicating successfully.

This text is largely focused on the legal foundations of law enforcement operations, so obviously, we view the role of legal advisors as critical to successful performance. We have found that there are two basic sets of attributes among attorneys involved in law enforcement legal advising. One set is legal procedure expertise, specifically the civil procedure matters related to litigation in (usually) the federal courts. These attorneys are a great resource when it comes to prevailing in litigation. They know the various ways in which their department client can be defended and how to use the "tricks of the trade" to get to the desired outcome. Other attorneys tend to be more familiar with law enforcement activities. They tend to be current or former prosecutors, law enforcement officers, or both. These attorneys will contribute a different type of knowledge to advising and teaching agency personnel; they know what it is like to work a night shift in an isolated rural area, or in the most troubled parts of an urban community, and how to assess and improve reports. They often communicate better with officers and other witnesses about the facts of a case. They may be better able to assess the worth of expert witness testimony, both for and against their client.

These two groups are not polar opposites. There is of course some degree of overlap among these sets of attributes. Each has a great deal of value to contribute to the agency and its protection. The "real world" of each is no less real than that of the other. Whether inside the agency or its governmental entity, provided by your insurance carrier, or otherwise accessible, all law enforcement agencies need to have access to these experts so as to maximize success in both enforcement activities and compliance with applicable legal standards and to reduce the risk to officers and the agency.

The patrol procedures/ control tactics (CT) instructors are also a critical component of the research and development process. These staff members contribute the ability to safely implement the legal authority described by legal personnel. There must be open communication, and some amount of joint research, between the patrol procedures staff and legal personnel. As a simple example, we all know that the use of force under the United States Constitutional standard must be "objectively reasonable." The decision as to what techniques are "objectively reasonable" under any particular set of circumstances is a mixed matter of both law and tactics. It is far better to attempt to discern the limits applicable and train accordingly than it is to retroactively try to create a basis for an officer's actions when the department and officer(s) are being scrutinized by any of a number of potentially hostile entities.

We suggest that provisions of a manual be laid out in logical progression, from the general to the specific. We also suggest that the authority for actions taken be provided specifically with each provision. This forces those responsible for researching and writing to consider the appropriate basis for actions directed or urged, and facilitates regular review and updating of provisions in the manual. Furthermore, we advocate cross-referencing to other provisions that may relate to the activity. It is our position that policies and procedures be used as performance improvement tools and that once validly drafted and tested, they become the foundation for on-going training.

One such provision might have the following general appearance:

POLICY # __-___ (Contacts/Investigative Detentions/Field Interviews(FI): General Category: Search and Seizure)
Authority: U.S. Constitution, 4th Amendment; State Constitution _____; State statute(s) _____
Related policy/procedure provisions: Investigative practices #___; Reports and Documentation #____; Use of Force/Subject Control #___; Dispatch Protocols #____).

Introduction: In performing law enforcement duties, officers encounter citizens under circumstances involving unusual conduct, some of which may indicate criminal activity. These circumstances span a wide variety of situations and conduct. Depending on the situation encountered, officer responses may range from a mere contact to a full-custody arrest.

Contacts: Face-to-face interaction between an officer and a citizen under circumstances where the citizen is free to leave if desired are often referred to as a "social contact." You may initiate a contact with a person in any place where you may lawfully be. A social contact is a good way to get to know the people of your patrol area, but it may also be undertaken when under the circumstances some investigation of an unusual (not necessarily suspicious) situation is appropriate. Persons who do not cooperate must be allowed to go on their way, may not be stopped or detained against their will or frisked (without more basis), and need not answer or cooperate. A officer is not authorized to utilize more coercive techniques unless he or she has a reasonable basis to believe that a crime is being committed, has been committed, or is about to be committed, as described below, **and** a reasonable basis to believe that the person to be stopped is suspected of participating in that offense.

The "field interview" and such investigative stops can be valuable components of a police officer's public safety and crime control efforts. Appropriate field interviews may provide opportunities to:

1. develop knowledge of a patrol area (people, places, and activities);
2. reduce opportunity for criminal conduct (crime suppression);
3. develop information regarding criminal activity, possibly leading to probable cause for arrest; and
4. demonstrate to the public a commitment to investigate suspicious circumstances.

There are two components to this practice: the "stop," which must be of reasonable and brief duration, and the "frisk," which allows an officer to protect him or herself by patting down the outer garments of the person stopped for weapons that might be used against the officer.

The field interview must be used with discretion and good judgment. It must be based on reasonable inferences from the circumstances encountered by the officer. Officers must be able to relate those observations that caused them to conclude that the person with whom you wish to speak is committing, about to commit, or has committed an offense. The analysis of the justification to stop a person must take into account the totality of the circumstances. Officers must have facts from which are drawn reasonable inferences, and these should lead to a reasonable suspicion that the person stopped is involved in criminal activity. These inferences are not certainties but reasonable conclusions based upon the facts and your professional experience.

A "stop" is a temporary detention of a person for investigation, a "seizure," and therefore subject to the requirements of the Fourth Amendment. A stop occurs when an officer uses his or her authority to compel a person to halt, remain in a particular place, or move a short distance to a nearby location, such as to use a radio or telephone or for identification purposes. Even a short movement will be reasonable only under limited circumstances, generally for identification, and only where the officer is in fact aware that a crime has actually occurred.

Stop Procedure/Implementation: If an officer reasonably infers from the circumstances that a person is committing, about to commit, or has committed an offense, you may stop that person, whether on foot or in a vehicle, in any public place. Officers must be prepared to cite those factors that lead to the belief that the stop was justified.

Factors that officers should consider when deciding to make a stop include, but may not be limited to:

1. Subject appearance—Does this person generally fit the description of a suspect in a known offense? Does this person fit your knowledge of persons generally encountered in this area? Are the person's clothes consistent with the weather and other conditions?

2. The subject's actions—Does this person appear to be fleeing? Is his or her behavior consistent with your knowledge of criminal activity? If so, what activity and behavior? Is he or she with others who by these factors also appear suspicious? Were conversations overheard that contributed to your suspicions?

3. Prior knowledge of the person—Does he or she have an arrest or conviction record, or does other credible information connect this person to criminal offenses? If so, does that information relate to offenses similar to the one believed to have occurred, or which is suspected to be about to occur? What other knowledge do you have about this person?

4. Demeanor during the contact—If the subject responded to questions during the contact, what was the nature of his or her answers? Were they evasive, suspicious on their own, or incriminating? What sort of non-verbal communication was displayed during the encounter?

5. Area of the stop—Is the subject near the area of a known crime soon after it occurred? Is the area known for high levels of criminal activity? Do the subject's actions or appearance match a type of crime for which the area is known?

6. Time of day—Is it unusual for people to be in the area at this time? Is it a time of day during which a certain type of crime is occurring, according to your knowledge or department intelligence?

7. Law enforcement training and experience (including personal and professional knowledge of the area)—Do this subject's appearance and behavior resemble a pattern followed in particular offenses? How does this subject's behavior compare to typical behavior in this particular area under similar conditions?

8. Law enforcement purpose—Are you investigating a specific crime, type of crime, or pattern of criminal activity? What type of crime?

9. Source of information—What is the basis for your suspicions? If part of the basis is information supplied by another person, what do you know about this person? Is he or she a criminal informant, a witness, or a crime victim? How credible is this person? Has he or she supplied reliable information in the past? How did this person obtain this information? Can you corroborate this information?

In making a stop, officer safety is of primary importance. Officers shall not make a stop if there is a basis to suspect that physical non-compliance is a significant possibility until and unless the ability to control the subject is established. You must ensure that you have and display such a sufficient and recognizable advantage that a potentially resistive or assaultive person is less willing to assault you. Officers shall notify dispatch of location, the description of the person being stopped, the person's name, vehicle license number or similar identification if known, and the nature of the circumstances. All such available information shall be given before initiating contact. Officers, dispatchers, and supervisory personnel are equally responsible for ensuring that sufficient information is given to dispatch. At least one backup unit shall be dispatched. Once sufficient information for a National Crime Information Center (NCIC) inquiry is obtained, it shall be relayed to dispatch for use in determining whether or not this person is wanted and in performing a criminal history inquiry. Warrant and criminal history inquiries shall be made at the earliest possible moment.

If the stop is related to the possible commission of a violent crime, including any assault, a weapons violation, involves stopping more than one person at a time, or any other situation that creates a reasonable possibility of physical non-compliance, officers shall wait for a backup officer before making contact.

Frisks: A "frisk" is a limited protective "search" for concealed weapons or dangerous instruments that may be used to attack the officer or another person. "Search" as used here is not the same kind of search made in an arrest situation or pursuant to a warrant. A "frisk" is generally limited to a patdown of the outer garments of the person stopped. The purpose of the frisk is not to discover evidence but for the protection of the officer. You may perform such a frisk at any time that the reasonable suspicion arises that you or another person are in danger of attack. If a reasonably cautious officer, under the circumstances, would believe that he or she or others in the area of the stop are in danger because the person stopped might be in possession of a weapon, then a frisk is justified. The same factors described above should be considered when making a decision about whether or not a frisk is appropriate. A frisk is not justified just because a stop is justified. The greater the potential for violence directed at officers as indicated by the crime or other circumstances, the greater the likelihood that a frisk will be appropriate.

Once the subject has been tactically approached and controlled, start the frisk on that part of the person's clothing most likely to be able to conceal a weapon or dangerous instrument. You may also frisk or secure any areas within the detained person's immediate reach if you reasonably suspect that such areas might contain a weapon. If, when conducting a frisk, you feel an object that you reasonably believe is a weapon, you may reach directly into that area of the person's clothing and remove the item. If the frisk does not disclose a weapon or other seizable item, you may now continue the investigation of the circumstances. Officers shall remain alert to the possibility of attack. The reasonableness of the length of the detention will depend on the circumstances encountered. If the subject is not arrested after the encounter, any items secured during the encounter are to be returned in a manner consistent with officer safety.

(**Note:** As the control techniques are completely described in another area of this text, they will not be replicated here. This is consistent with the practice we advocate with regard to your department manual, as you can tell by our advocacy of cross-referencing manual provisions as shown in the header.)

Opposite-sex frisks: There is no legal requirement that subjects be frisked by an officer of the same sex. However, to the extent feasible and consistent with officer safety under the circumstances encountered, officers are encouraged to refrain from frisking subjects of the opposite sex if an officer of the same sex as the subject is reasonably available.

Documentation: Officers shall complete the department FI form (including any related use of force documentation if your agency uses such forms) prior to the end of the shift in which the FI was conducted unless an arrest results from the FI, in which case the arrest report shall be completed.

Index

Page numbers in italic indicate a figure on the corresponding page.